Conquerors for Christ

Scriptural

Kingdom Authority & Power Principles

For

God's Kings & Priests

In the Marketplace & Beyond,

In Their Daily Lives

Volume 1

Michael James Robertson

Copyright © 2006 by Michael James Robertson

Conquerors For Christ
by Michael James Robertson

Printed in the United States of America

ISBN 1-60034-503-4

All rights reserved solely by the author. The author guarantees all contents are original and do not infringe upon the legal rights of any other person or work. No part of this book may be reproduced in any form without the permission of the author. The views expressed in this book are not necessarily those of the publisher.

Unless otherwise indicated, Bible quotations are taken from the King James Version of the Bible. Copyright © 1988 by Thomas Nelson Publishers.

www.xulonpress.com

Dedication

I dedicate this manuscript to My Lord and Savior Jesus Christ and to His Faithful Remnant around the whole of the world — His kings and priests — His Army of the Light — His Conquerors for Christ — that shall finish the work of the Father by executing the "Great Commission" of Jesus Christ! All Glory to God! Hallelujah! Amen and Amen! **"Jesus saith unto them, My meat is to do the will of Him that sent Me, and to finish His work."** (John 4:34 KJV).

Forward

"<u>Conquerors for Christ</u> is a must read for Christian businessmen. In his new book, Michael Robertson presents a high energy... and motivational piece. Regardless of where you stand in your walk of faith with Christ, this is a pertinent presentation...Robertson knows his scripture and is a highly effective motivational writer. <u>Conquerors for Christ</u> is cutting edge biblical scholarship...I found myself making notes in the margins after every paragraph and thinking: "Wow, this is great!" I highly recommend the book to everyone, but especially those who are tired of hearing the cultural pundits proclaim the concept of the Christian businessmen has become an oxymoron...Michael Robertson recognizes the relevance of the Christian businessman and reminds us of the role we need to play. It is very refreshing!"

C. Alan Walker,
President & CEO
Bradford Coal Co., Inc.

"After reading <u>Conquerors for Christ</u> it further reinforced my perception of what is happening today in the market place with believers... called to work diligently and be faithful and honest in all of our business affairs...but there is so much more that is available to us in the Word of God to exemplify to a lost and dying world within the market place! We are to conquer the market place not just in creative business plans but also with the delegated authority as our Father's kings and priests on the earth.

Michael, you have hit the sweet spot for believers who are called to evangelize their mission field of today's market place and the Scriptures you have woven carefully together in this treatise makes excellent reading on a daily basis! Listen market place conquerors, this treatise you will want to keep close to your desk and read over and over as you wait on the Holy Spirit for courage and direction to do unusual exploits for His glory in this exciting hour! Glory to God!"

Scott M. Holtz
President
Rivers in the Desert International

"Michael Robertson's <u>Conquerors for Christ</u> is a clear call for every believer to step into the public square. The Scriptural Kingdom Authority Principles gleaned from the Bible can be powerfully applied in the marketplace. <u>Conquerors for Christ</u> is a catalyst to see anointed men and women rise up and penetrate society to the glory of God. May God use it greatly for His Kingdom!"

Rev. Peter D. McIntosh
Senior Pastor
Kennedy Road Tabernacle

Contents

1. Introduction: xi
   Who Are They? xi
   Where Are They? xii
   How Will I Recognize Them? xii
   How Can I Become One? xiii
   Scriptural Kingdom Authority & Power Principles xiii
2. Integrity in Christ 17
3. Crucified with Christ & Changed into His Image 23
4. Our Vision & Goals 31
5. Discipline to Disciple – Terms of Discipleship 37
6. Loyalty, Unity, Esprit de Corps 45
7. Influence Our World & Enforce the Victory of Christ 51
8. Leadership – Showing "The Way" 59
9. Faithful Stewardship 67
10. Passion – The Fire of the Holy Ghost 73
11. Our Greatest Destiny & Highest Nobility 77
12. Our Most Significant Responsibility 81
13. More on Responsibility to Jesus 87
14. Kingdom Authority 93

15. Evangelizing, Discipleship & Witnessing.............................103
16. Faithful Obedience...111
17. His Service – The Road Best Traveled 115
18. Why Ambassadors for Jesus Christ Are Relevant................121
19. Declare the Evangel 127
20. Honor: Our Key to Evangelism & Discipleship 131
21. Christ Jesus & the Affairs of Men...135
22. Heroic Spirit of Christ..141
23. More on Active, Violent Faith...145
24. Courageous for Christ..151
25. Our Vision/Mission – The "Great Commission" 157
26. Commitment, Devotion, Loyalty – All or Nothing..............165
27. Whom Shall I Send? 173
28. Architects of Heroes for Christ 183
29. Shepherds for Christ 189
30. Valor in Humility 195
31. Christ's Character Is Our Destiny 203
32. COMMITMENT TO ACTION..209
33. Contact Us & In Re: Volume 2 213

Introduction

Who Are They?

"Conquerors for Christ" are individuals who are born again in the precious blood of Jesus Christ. "Conquerors for Christ" are anointed individuals who are passionately in love with our Lord and Savior! These Soldiers of the Cross of Christ have committed their time, treasure and talent to living the life to which Christ has called and chosen them. "Conquerors for Christ" exalt Jesus Christ above all else and are committed to the Kingdom Authority and Power of the Word of God! "Conquerors for Christ" are faithful, at all cost, in advancing and executing the "Great Commission" of our King of kings and Lord of lords in the marketplace and beyond, in their daily lives. These ambassadors for Christ claim their rightful Kingdom Authority and Power and enforce the victory of His Cross and the power of His Resurrection by asserting the power of God through their violent active faith against the adversary, sin, sickness, death, false preachers, prophets and teachers in the apostate church, and the ways of the world. Their responsibility is to persevere in diligently seeking the Kingdom of God and all of its manifestations, hungering and thirsting for all of the authority, power and presence of the Holy Spirit in their lives and in the church, which is the body of Christ. These kings and priests of Christ Jesus take hold of the Kingdom of Heaven by force and are committed to break away from sinful practices as they relentlessly pursue Christ, His righteousness, which is His character and image, and the Kingdom Authority and Power of His Word! "Conquerors for Christ" live a lifestyle of repentance — a lifestyle of REVIVAL! As such, "Conquerors for

Christ" are the faithful executors, stewards and trustees of the faith, and hence, of the Gospel of Jesus Christ our Lord! Hallelujah!

Where Are They?

"Conquerors for Christ" are mighty men, women and children of Almighty God who are found in all walks of life and in every corner of the world. They exert their Kingdom Authority and Power by demonstrating and proclaiming the Gospel of Jesus Christ to their fellow men, women and children via their particular language and cultural and ethnic heritage. The eternal and universal truth of the Cross of Christ and the power of His Resurrection is the banner (Jehovah Nissi) under which they march as the Soldiers of the Cross, and of the Army of the Light! "Conquerors for Christ" are revived afresh and anew every day with the infilling of the Holy Spirit, as they exude the very countenance of Christ and His Kingdom Authority and Power, in their daily pursuit to apprehend even more of His holy character! All Glory to God!

How Will I Recognize Them?

"Conquerors for Christ" all live by the same ethic and principle, which is the Kingdom Authority and Power of the Holy Bible. When you meet them you will sense that there is something different about them — something you would like to have — the unconditional love, fierce courage and perfect integrity that come from true freedom, authority and power in the victory of Jesus Christ. The very joy, light, presence and strength of Christ Jesus permeate and radiate from their being, as they live their own personal revival in the glory and power of the Holy Spirit! Daily, "Conquerors for Christ" hold high the Cross of Christ as they bear the fruit of the Holy Spirit and manifest His gifts and power in the service of Christ's Army of the Light. Thus, "Conquerors for Christ" enforce the victory of Christ by asserting His Kingdom Authority and Power over the enemy, sin, sickness, death, false preachers, prophets and teachers in the apostate church, and the ways of the world. The battle cry of "Conquerors for Christ" is: "Give us souls lest we die, that the Lamb who was slain might receive the reward of His suffering, as the glory perfects the unity, and the unity proclaims the glory!" Hallelujah!

How Can I Become One?

Anyone can become a "Conqueror for Christ". All you need to do is repent of your sins, invite Jesus Christ into your heart as Lord and Savior, and commit yourself to His teachings. He will reveal Himself to you in very special ways as you embark upon the process of becoming the person He has called and chosen you to be, by the Kingdom Authority and Power of the Cross of Christ and the Resurrection and Revival Power of the Holy Spirit! Say this prayer right now and mean it with all of your heart: "Father God, I know that I am a sinner. I repent from my sins and I ask You to forgive me of my sins. Jesus Christ, You died for me on the Cross. Jesus, I believe that God raised You from the dead. Jesus, I confess You as Lord of my life. I invite You, Jesus, into my heart. Please come into my heart and save me, Jesus! Thank You, Jesus; I am born again in Your precious blood, by the power of the Holy Spirit. Jesus, I belong to You forevermore! And Jesus, I ask You to make me a mighty "Conqueror for Christ"! Amen!" Congratulations! We welcome you to Jesus Christ's Army of the Light as you join His mighty Brigade of "Conquerors for Christ"! Hallelujah!

Scriptural Kingdom Authority & Power Principles

> "And this Gospel of the Kingdom shall be preached in all the world for a witness unto all nations; and then shall the end come." (Matthew 24:14 KJV).

"Conquerors for Christ" is a dynamic, vigorous and ongoing treatise of Christ-centered Kingdom Authority and Power Principles, which arm Soldiers of the Cross of Jesus Christ with the fundamental biblical authority necessary to pursue the love and character of Christ Jesus, daily. We are in the last days! Witness the fact that in 1948 Israel once again became a nation, as well as the current unrest and violence between Israel and the Palestinian terrorists; witness the great apostasy and false preachers, prophets and teachers that rife throughout the church of Jesus Christ, along with the attendant breakdown of Kingdom Authority and increase in lawlessness; witness the socio-religious climate that portends a one world church; witness the various severe famines and pestilence around the world; witness the change in the jet stream; witness the hole in the ozone layer; witness global warming ; witness the severity of the hurricanes, tornados and other violent storms; witness the number and magnitude of earthquakes around the world and the resultant tidal waves; witness the explosion of the population and the attendant starvation; witness the proliferation of nuclear weapons in the Middle East and North Korea; witness the abominable evil and heinous terrorism manifested by radical Islam throughout the world. The devil and his demons have the world on the precipice of annihilation from the diabolical evil they confidently flaunt and perpetrate, and billions of lost and dying souls are at stake, here at home, as well as around the world! The church desperately needs REVIVAL! "Conquerors for Christ" is the clarion call for the end time REVIVAL of the church of Jesus Christ — one by one, soldier by soldier, fellowship by fellowship and church by church! When we purpose to pursue Christ with all that we are, we die to self daily by going back through the Cross of Christ, thus yielding to the Holy Spirit, which allows Christ to flow forth from our bellies as rivers of living water in blessing, victory and resurrection life! We live a lifestyle of repentance — a lifestyle of REVIVAL, because we live in the humility, contriteness, sacrificial love and obedience of Christ Jesus, Himself! Therefore, we live and manifest all of His Kingdom Authority and Power, and through the Power of the Holy Spirit, we live and manifest our personal REVIVAL!

"Conquerors for Christ" prepares each of us for the battle at hand against the enemy of the Cross of Christ by arming us with the defensive and offensive weaponry and the requisite Kingdom Authority and Power necessary to enforce the victory of Jesus Christ in the marketplace and beyond, in our daily lives. Our prophetic destiny, as the kings and priests of Jesus Christ and of the Kingdom of God on this earth, is to reign on the earth, thereby making provision for His vision by earning income to support His Covenant and church, as well as proclaiming the Gospel of Jesus Christ in all nations. "Conquerors for Christ" imparts unto its readers the empowering, overcoming and triumphant truths of success and significance, with which to defeat the adversary at every turn, from the ultimate source, our Lord and Savior Jesus Christ! These eternal Kingdom Authority and Power principles and truths provide for, and when properly executed ensure, our victory in the war for the harvest of lost souls in these last days! Even now, as the number of "Conquerors for Christ" continues to grow and increase, witnessing more and more Soldiers of the Cross of Christ being empowered to live personal revival on a daily basis, Jesus Christ is uniting us together, around the whole of the world, under the sacred blood stained banner of the Cross of Christ, as the Faithful Remnant and the end time Army of the Light, to lead the last days revival of the church of Jesus Christ! What say you? Will you answer this clarion call from the King of kings, and the Lord of lords? All Glory to God! Hallelujah! Let us move forward, then, with all dispatch, and faithfully execute the "Great Commission" of our Lord and Savior Jesus Christ! As we move out and take our prophetically assigned and ordained positions in the marketplace and beyond, in our daily lives, let us call to mind and proclaim the battle cry of "Conquerors for Christ"; "Give us souls lest we die, that the Lamb who was slain might receive the reward of His suffering, as the glory perfects the unity, and the unity proclaims the glory!" Amen! **"And I, if I be lifted up from the earth, will draw all men unto Me." (John 12: 32 KJV).**

Integrity in Christ

As Christian men and women, and as God's kings and priests, we have been granted a prophetic destiny and purpose — a divine standing order — a holy Commission — the "Great Commission". Christ Jesus has chosen us to be His kings and priests and we have taken our stand in the marketplace and beyond, in our daily lives. We must never waiver from the responsibility of assuming our stand because we are Christ's line of conquest, and we know that Almighty God's plan is perfect and we have active, violent faith in His end. We must never look back! We must continue to press into and apprehend our Christ Jesus, which is our goal and purpose on this earth! We must never let go of Cross of Christ! Therefore, let us take up our cross, daily, and follow Him! Hallelujah! **"Wherefore take unto you the whole armor of God, that ye may be able to withstand in the evil day, and having done all, to stand." (Ephesians 6:13 KJV). "Not as though I had already attained, either were already perfect: but I follow after, if that I may apprehend that for which also I am apprehended of Christ Jesus." (Philippians 3:12 KJV). "No man, having put his hand to the plough, and looking back, is fit for the Kingdom of God." (Luke 9:62 KJV). "If any man will come after me, let him deny himself, and take up his cross daily, and follow Me." (Luke 9:23 KJV).**

As we creatively, passionately and vigorously engage our opportunity for Christ in the marketplace and beyond, in our daily lives, we must explore Almighty God's Word to discover the principles He has provided for us to be faithful, significant and successful executors, ministers, stewards and trustees of the faith, and hence, of the Gospel of Jesus Christ. We must then activate our violent faith and live the very righteousness of Christ Jesus. We must walk the talk! This goes to our integrity, which is our ethical value of moral wholeness — of consistency between ethic, principle and practice. Therefore, being children of God with integrity means that we make our decisions with the Holy Spirit based upon biblical principles, and then we demonstrate, exercise and practice our decisions through our active, violent faith. We demonstrate, exercise and practice Almighty God's Word! We are moral to our ethic and principle, thus we are people of integrity. We live Jesus! We are changed into His image and character! There has to be a balance — a reciprocity between our hearing and believing Almighty God's Word, and our doing God's Word. This constitutes our integrity. **"Even so faith, if it hath not works is dead, being alone...I will show thee my faith by my works." (James 2:17, 18 KJV). "...[T]he Kingdom of Heaven suffereth violence, and the violent take it by force." (Matthew 11:12 KJV). "For He hath made Him to be sin for us, who knew no sin; that we might be made the righteousness of God in Him." (2 Corinthians 5:21 KJV). "But we all, with open face beholding as in a glass the glory of the Lord, are changed into the same image from glory to glory, even as by the Spirit of the Lord." (2 Corinthians 3:18 KJV). "Let me be weighed in an even balance, that God may know mine integrity." (Job 31:6 KJV). "The Lord shall judge the people: judge me, O Lord, according to my righteousness and according to mine integrity that is in me." (Psalm 7:8 KJV).**

Our Sovereign Father has bequeathed unto us a blessed and fulfilling opportunity to make a significant difference for Jesus Christ here upon this earth. Ours is an exciting opportunity, to be sure. But opportunity without action produces nothing. Only by acting upon our God-given opportunity are we able to experience its awesome potential. Our integrity requires the moral courage to do what is right, to stand up and be counted, and to diligently demonstrate the courage of our beliefs and convictions in our Lord Jesus Christ. Opportunities need to be seized — made the most of — taken advantage of! Let us boldly and bravely seize our opportunity for Jesus Christ! Let us be determined, by our active, violent faith, to bear holy fruit as co-laborers with Christ, thereby reaping the full harvest of souls in our "Great Commission" for Christ! **"He becometh poor that dealeth with a slack hand: but the hand of the diligent maketh rich." (Proverbs 10:4 KJV). "And whatsoever ye do, do it heartily, as to the Lord...for ye serve the Lord Christ." (Colossians 3:23,24 KJV). "Wherefore by their fruits ye shall know them." (Matthew 7:20 KJV). "...The harvest truly is plenteous, but the laborers are few: Pray ye therefore the Lord of the harvest, that He will send forth laborers into His harvest." (Matthew 9:37, 38 KJV).**

The marketplace and beyond, in our daily lives, is Father God's platform to launch and sustain the revival of the Cross of Christ and the power of His Resurrection from the local grassroots business and commerce centers of our neighborhoods and around the world. He has placed us in the vital and commanding position to support His Covenant and to spread the Gospel of Jesus Christ by being faithful to our "Great Commission". **"Go ye into all the world, and preach the Gospel to every creature." (Mark 16:15 KJV).** Let us harvest precious hearts, souls and spirits for Jesus! Let us live by integrity and activate our "Great Commission"! **"...All power is given unto Me in heaven and in earth. Go ye therefore, and teach all nations, baptizing them in the Name of the Father, and of the Son, and of the Holy Ghost: Teaching them to observe all things whatsoever I have commanded you: and, lo, I am with you always, even unto the end of the world. Amen." (Matthew 28:18-20 KJV).**

Our integrity conforms our reality to our word — it fulfills that which we proclaim is our ethic and principle. We have enlisted in the Army of the Light as soldiers of the Cross of Jesus Christ. Hence, we are serving God in the marketplace and beyond, in our daily lives, as His new creations and redeemed individuals, having been washed in the blood of Jesus Christ. As such, we are His Kingdom — His church — the ecclesia (the called out ones) — the Body of Christ — the Army of the Light! It is our responsibility to nurture our faith and develop our integrity by the Word of God, so that we can be the light of the world, continually radiating His glory through our persevering and persistent action! **"Ye are the light of the world. A city that is set on a hill cannot be hid...Let your light so shine before** men, that they may see your good works, and glorify your Father which is in Heaven." (Matthew 5:14, 16 KJV). "Rise, shine, for thy light is come, and the glory of the Lord is risen upon thee. For behold, the darkness shall cover the earth and gross darkness the people: but the Lord shall rise upon thee, and His glory shall be seen upon thee. And the Gentiles shall come to thy light, and kings to the brightness of thy rising." (Isaiah 60:1-3 KJV).

As "Conquerors for Christ" and kings and priests of the Gospel of Jesus Christ, we are appointed and chosen for the defense and confirmation of the integrity of the Gospel! Our Lord and Savior Jesus Christ has committed the truth of His Gospel to our trust! We are the executors, stewards and trustees of the last will and testament of the King of kings and Lord of lords! Our supreme duty is to contend for the integrity of the faith, at all cost, by asserting the power of God against the adversary, sin, sickness, death, false preachers, prophets and teachers in the apostate church, and the ways of the world! Our "Great Commission" is to batter down and breakthrough the gates of hell with the Cross of Christ, by preaching Christ and Him crucified and the power of the Resurrection to a lost and dying world, as well as to a backslidden and apostate church. Our faithfulness and integrity in Christ Jesus demand that we expose sin, both within and without the camp, by shining the Light of Christ's Gospel into the darkness of the enemy's domain. "...[A]nd in the defense and confirmation of the Gospel, ye are partakers of my grace". (Philippians 1:7 KJV). "...[K]nowing that I am set for the defense of the Gospel.". (Philippians 1:17 KJV). "According to the glorious Gospel of the blessed God, which was committed to my trust." (1 Timothy 1:11 KJV). "O Timothy, keep that which was committed to thy trust...." (1 Timothy 6:20 KJV). "Beloved, when I gave all diligence to write unto you of the common salvation, it was needful for me to write unto you, and exhort you that ye should earnestly contend for the faith which was once delivered unto the saints." (Jude 3 KJV). "...Woe is unto me if I preach not the Gospel." (1 Corinthians 9:16 KJV). "Let no man deceive you by any means: for that day shall not come, except there come a falling away first, and that man of sin be revealed, the son of perdition." (2 Thessalonians 2:3 KJV). "...[T]he Kingdom of Heaven suffereth violence, and the violent take it by force." (Matthew 11:12 KJV). "...[U]pon this rock I will build My church; and the gates of hell shall not prevail against it." (Matthew 16:18 KJV). "For I have determined not to know anything among you, save Jesus Christ and Him crucified." (2 Corinthians 2:2 KJV). "For the preaching of the Cross...is the power of God." (1 Corinthians 1:18 KJV). "But we preach Christ crucified...Christ the power of God and the wisdom of God." (1 Corinthians 1:23, 24 KJV). "And the city had no need of the sun, neither of the moon, to shine in it: for the glory of God did lighten it, and the Lamb is the light thereof." (Revelation 21:23 KJV).

O God, our daily prayer is that we may walk our talk by creatively, passionately and vigorously demonstrating our integrity as your kings and priests in the marketplace and beyond, in our daily lives, through our active, violent faith in the promise of Jesus Christ. **"And hath made us kings and priests unto God and His Father; to Him be glory and dominion for ever and ever. Amen." (Revelation 1:6 KJV).** Father, have us be successful and significant in your eyes and bless our actions of our testimony of Christ Jesus on this earth as you honor our actions of the same in heaven. Imbue us and infill us with the overcoming power of the Holy Spirit so that we faithfully speak with Jesus' words, act with Jesus' actions and shine with Jesus' light in all that we do! Have us take our stand as victorious Soldiers of the Cross of Christ and "Conquerors for Christ" in the marketplace and beyond, in our daily lives, with the utmost of the integrity of the faith and Gospel of Jesus Christ! In the precious Name of Jesus, we pray and apprehend! Amen! Hallelujah! **"And they overcame him with the blood of the Lamb, and by the Word of their testimony..." (Revelation 12:11 KJV). These shall make war with the Lamb, and the Lamb shall overcome them: for He is Lord of lords, and King of kings: and they that are with Him are called, and chosen, and faithful." (Revelation 17:14 KJV). "Nay, in all these things we are more than conquerors through Him that loved us." (Romans 8:37 KJV). "And hath made us unto our God kings and priests: and we shall reign on the earth." (Revelation 5:10 KJV).**

"But they that wait upon the Lord shall renew their strength; they shall mount up with wings as eagles; they shall run, and not be weary; and they shall walk, and not faint." (Isaiah 40:31 KJV).

Crucified with Christ & Changed into His Image

"**I am crucified with Christ: nevertheless I live; yet not I, but Christ liveth in me: and the life which I now live in the flesh, I live by the faith of the Son of God, who loved me and gave Himself for me." (Galatians 2:20 KJV).** In order to become born again we must come to the end of ourselves and repent of our sins. We must purpose to turn away from our sin in favor of Christ. We must die to self, pride, sin, sin nature, the enemy, our desires and the ways of the world. We must empty ourselves of self and everything else, but Christ. When we die to self, we live to Christ. His life and Spirit live through us. Through the offense and death of self in the Cross of Christ, we secure supernatural life in the Holy Spirit of God. This assures our translation to Christ by identifying us in His crucifixion, Resurrection and eternal life! What is more, Christ Jesus commands us to go back through His Cross daily. Only by going back to the Cross daily, are we able to live a life-style of repentance. Only by dying to self and living to Christ Jesus daily, are we able to realize that, with Christ all things are possible, and without Him, we are nothing. Christ knows our humanity. We must be reminded of the same daily, as we go back through the Cross of Christ. In this way, we pursue life in the Spirit of God by living the virtues of humility, contriteness, sacrificial love and obedience. These are the terms of discipleship! Thus, we become crucified unto the world, and the world unto us, for the sake of Christ and His Gospel! Daily, we are empowered to hold high our great standard — Jehovah Nisi — the blood stained banner of the Cross of Christ! Hallelujah! "...[T]he offense of the cross..." (Galatians

5:11 KJV). "As it is written, Behold, I lay in Zion a stumbling stone and rock of offense: and whosoever believeth on Him shall not be ashamed." (Romans 9:33 KJV). "Knowing this, that our old man is crucified with Him...we shall be also in the likeness of His Resurrection...alive unto God through Jesus Christ our Lord." (Romans 6:6, 5, 11 KJV). "And He said unto them all, If any man will come after Me, let him deny Himself, and take up His cross daily, and follow Me." (Luke 9:23 KJV). "And He that taketh not His cross, and followeth after Me, is not worthy of Me." (Matthew 10:38 KJV). "And whosoever doeth not bear His cross, and come after Me, cannot be My disciple." (Luke 14:27 KJV). "I can do all things through Christ which strengtheneth me." (Philippians 4:13 KJV). "And hath raised us up together, and made us sit together in heavenly places in Christ Jesus." (Ephesians 2:6 KJV). "But God forbid that I should glory, save in the cross of our Lord Jesus Christ, by whom the world is crucified unto me, and I unto the world." (Galatians 6:14 KJV). "From henceforth let no man trouble me: for I bear in my body the marks of the Lord Jesus." (Galatians 6:17 KJV). "...When the enemy shall come in like a flood, the Spirit of the Lord shall raise up a standard against him." (Isaiah 59:19 KJV).

When we go through the Cross of Christ and become born again in His shed blood, supernaturally, we become new creatures in Christ by the power of the Holy Spirit. We are imbued with a new vision by which to live our lives. When the Holy Spirit of the living God indwells our bodies, He gives us the exousia authority of Christ to breakthrough all of the old, stale, mediocre, sinful and status quo ways of doing things. The anointing of the Holy Spirit empowers us to change in dramatic, revolutionary and transforming ways into the character and image of Christ. We now have all of the authority of Christ to be just like Him. We have a new vision, and that new vision is of life lived in the victory of Christ Jesus! Hallelujah! **"Therefore if any man be in Christ, he is a new creature, old things are passed away; behold all things are become new." (2 Corinthians 5:17 KJV). "What? Know ye not that your body is the temple of the Holy Ghost which is in you, which ye have of God, and ye are not your own?" (1 Corinthians 6:19 KJV). "And be not** conformed to this world: but be transformed by the renewing of your mind, that ye may prove what is that good, and acceptable, and perfect, will of God." (Romans 12:2 KJV). "Behold, I give unto you power to tread on serpents and scorpions, and over all the power of the enemy: and nothing shall by any means hurt you." (Luke 10:19 KJV). "Where there is no vision, the people perish." (Proverbs 29:18 KJV). "And the Lord answered me and said, Write the vision, and make it plain upon the tables, that he may run that readeth it." (Habakkuk 2:2 KJV). "But thanks be to God, which giveth us the victory through our Lord Jesus Christ." (1 Corinthians 15:57 KJV).

As "Conquerors for Christ", we are free in the liberty of Christ to pursue His very character and image. Indeed, the purpose of Father God for every born again believer is to become conformed to the image of His Son, Jesus Christ! We do this by unceasingly focusing and looking unto Christ Jesus in prayer, praise and thanksgiving, as well as by constantly and consistently feeding our spirits by the washing of the Word of God. By the power and unction of the Holy Ghost, we become changed into the character and image of Christ Jesus from glory to glory. This is the process of sanctification and holiness — of bearing the fruit of the Spirit, which is the very character of our Lord and Savior Jesus Christ! **"Stand fast therefore in the liberty wherewith Christ has made us free, and be not entangled again with the yoke of bondage." (Galatians 5:1 KJV). "And we know that all things work together for good to them that love God, to them that are called according to His purpose. For whom He did foreknow, He also did predestinate to be conformed to the image of His Son, that He might be the firstborn among many brethren." (Romans 8:28, 29 KJV). "Looking unto Jesus the Author and Finisher of our faith; who for the joy that was set before Him endured the cross, despising the shame, and is set down at the right hand of the throne of God." (Hebrews 12:2 KJV). "Rejoice evermore. Pray without ceasing. In every thing give thanks: for this is the will of God in Christ Jesus concerning you." (1 Thessalonians 5:16-18 KJV). "That He might sanctify and cleanse it with the washing of water by the Word." (Ephesians 5:26 KJV). "Now the Lord is that Spirit:**

and where the Spirit of the Lord is, there is liberty. But we all, with open face beholding as in a glass the glory of the Lord, are changed into the same image from glory to glory, even as by the Spirit of the Lord." (2 Corinthians 3:17, 18 KJV). "Because it is written, Be ye holy; for I am holy." (1 Peter 1:16 KJV). "But the fruit of the Spirit is love, joy, peace, longsuffering, gentleness, goodness, faith, meekness, temperance: against such there is no law." (Galatians 5:22, 23 KJV).

The more we press into Christ Jesus, the more we bear the fruit of the Spirit. The more we are changed into the character and image of Christ by bearing His fruit, the more we grow in His agape love. Agape love is the unconditional and unmerited love of the Father, Son and Holy Spirit, which is the very sacrificial love that constrained the Lamb of God, Jesus Christ, to the Cross, as the perfect Sacrifice offered by the perfect High Priest, for your sin and mine. It is this great agape, sacrificial love, which constrains "Conquerors for Christ" to do the work of Jesus Christ by proclaiming His Gospel to a lost and dying world, as well as to a backslidden and apostate church. The more we are changed into the image of Christ from glory to glory by demonstrating His humility, contriteness, sacrificial love and obedience, the more the Holy Spirit manifests through us with the power of the gifts of the Spirit. We must remember that the condition precedent to the manifestation of the gifts of the Spirit is the Baptism of the Holy Spirit. This provides us with the dunamis, dynamite power to do the work of Christ. **"And when the day of Pentecost was fully come, they were all with one accord in one place. And suddenly there came a sound from Heaven as of a rushing mighty wind, and it filled all the house where they were sitting. And there appeared unto them cloven tongues like as fire, and it sat upon each of them. And they were all filled with the Holy Ghost, and began to speak in other tongues, as the Spirit gave them utterance...And it shall come to pass in the last days, saith God, I will pour out of My Spirit upon all flesh: and your sons and your daughters shall prophesy, and your young men shall see visions, and your old men shall dream dreams... And I will show wonders in Heaven above, and signs in the earth beneath...And it shall come to pass, that whosoever shall call** on the Name of the Lord shall be saved." (Acts 2:1-4, 17, 19, 21 KJV).** The purpose of the gifts of the Spirit is to assert the power of God against the adversary, sin, sickness, death, the apostate church, and the ways of the world. This is realized by the manifestation of the Holy Spirit via signs, wonders and miracles, through the active, fierce, unrelenting, and violent faith of the Faithful Remnant and Soldiers of the Cross of Jesus Christ — the "Conquerors for Christ"! We are the chosen enforcers of the victory of the Cross of Christ and the power of His Resurrection! Hallelujah! Our responsibility is to seek first the kingdom of God and His righteousness. We are to persevere in diligently seeking all of the presence, power and authority of Christ Jesus in our lives and in the church. We are consummately committed to breakthrough sinful practices, while exalting Christ in all things and recommitting to the authority and power of His Word! All Glory to God! As debtors to Christ Jesus, who is our spiritual creditor, our spiritual honor and duty is to fulfill our debt to Christ Jesus in relation to every lost soul! We are constrained to do everything that is commanded in the Word of God to prepare the way for — to enable — Christ to bring His redemption into evident reality in the lives of others, through us, His ambassadors in bonds, kings and priests, and "Conquerors for Christ"! Thus, we shall hasten the return of the Lord Jesus Christ. Amen! **" God is love." (1 John 4:16 KJV). "For God so loved the world, that He gave His only begotten Son, that whosoever believeth in Him should not perish, but have everlasting life." (John 3:16 KJV). "Greater love hath no man than this, that a man lay down His life for His friends." (John 15:13 KJV). "But God commendeth His love toward us, in that, while we were still sinners, Christ died for us." (Romans 5:8 KJV). "...[T]he love of God is shed abroad in our hearts by the Holy Ghost which is given unto us." (Romans 5:5 KJV). "For the love of Christ constraineth us; because we thus judge, that if one died for all, then were all dead. And that He died for all, that they which live should not hence forth live unto themselves, but unto Him which died for them, and rose again." (2 Corinthians 5:14, 15 KJV). "For I am not ashamed of the Gospel of Christ: for it is the power of God unto salvation to everyone that believeth..." (Romans 1:16 KJV). "And,** behold, I send the promise of My Father upon you: but tarry ye in the city of Jerusalem, until ye be endued with power from on high." (Luke 24:49 KJV). "But the manifestation of the Spirit is given to every man to profit withal. For to one is given by the Spirit the word of wisdom; to another the word of knowledge by the same Spirit; To another faith by the same Spirit; to another the gifts of healing by the same Spirit; To another the working of miracles; to another prophecy; to another discerning of spirits; to another divers tongues; to another the interpretation of tongues." (1 Corinthians 12:7-10 KJV). "...[T]he Kingdom of Heaven suffereth violence, and the violent take it by force." (Matthew 11:12 KJV). "Behold, I give you power to tread on serpents and scorpions, and over all the power of the enemy: and nothing shall by any means hurt you." (Luke 10:19 KJV). "And having spoiled principalities and powers, He made a show of them openly, triumphing over them in it." (Colossians 2:15 KJV). "Ye have not chosen Me, but I have chosen you, and ordained you, that ye should go and bring forth fruit, and that your fruit should remain: that whatsoever ye shall ask of the Father in My Name, He shall give it to you." (John 15:16 KJV). "These shall make war with the Lamb, and the Lamb shall overcome them: for He is Lord of lords, and King of kings: and they that are with him are called, and chosen, and faithful." (Revelation 17:14 KJV). "But thanks be to God, which giveth us the victory through our Lord Jesus Christ." (1 Corinthians 15:57 KJV). "Now thanks be unto God, which always causeth us to triumph in Christ, and maketh manifest the savor of His knowledge by us in every place." (2 Corinthians 2:14 KJV). "But seek ye first the Kingdom of God, and His righteousness: and all these things shall be added unto you." (Matthew 6:33 KJV). "And He is Head of the body, the church: who is the beginning, the first-born from the dead; that in all things He might have the pre-eminence." (Colossians 1:18 KJV). "All scripture is given by inspiration of God, and is profitable for doctrine, for reproof, for correction, for instruction in righteousness: that the man of God may be perfect, thoroughly furnished unto all good works." (2 Timothy 3:16, 17 KJV). "I am a debtor both to the Greeks, and to the Barbarians; both to the wise, and to the unwise." (Romans 1:14 KJV). "Now then we are ambassadors for Christ, as though God did beseech you by us: we pray you in Christ's stead, be ye reconciled to God." (2 Corinthians 5:20 KJV)."But ye shall receive power, after that the Holy Ghost is come upon you: and ye shall be witnesses unto Me both in Jerusalem, and all of Judea, and in Samaria, and unto the uttermost part of the earth." (Acts 1:8 KJV). "And hast made us unto our God kings and priests: and we shall reign on the earth." (Revelation 5:10 KJV). "Nay, in all these things we are more than conquerors through Him who loved us." (Romans 8:37 KJV). "Looking for and hasting unto the coming of the day of God..." (2 Peter 3:12 KJV).

> "But they that wait upon the Lord shall renew their strength; they shall mount up with wings as eagles; they shall run, and not be weary; and they shall walk, and not faint." (Isaiah 40:31 KJV).

Our Vision & Goals

"Where there is no vision the people perish..." (Proverbs 29:18 KJV).

As "Conquerors for Christ", it is incumbent upon each of us to create a vision statement, in writing, which expresses the will of Father God, as given unto us by the Holy Spirit. **"And the Lord answered me, and said, Write the vision, and make it plain upon the tables, that he may run that readeth it." (Habakkuk 2:2 KJV).** Said vision statement serves to keep us focused on the perfect will of the Father, thus advancing the Kingdom of His Son. If we discern through the Holy Spirit that our vision is not congruent with Almighty God's plan for us in His "Great Commission", then we must summon the courage and wherewithal to change our vision, consistent with the power and wisdom of the Holy Spirit. **"I can do all things through Christ which strengtheneth me." (Philippians 4:13 KJV). "And the Spirit of the Lord shall rest upon him, the Spirit of wisdom and understanding, the Spirit of counsel and might, the Spirit of knowledge and of fear of the Lord." (Isaiah 11:2 KJV). "...Not by might, nor by power, but by My Spirit, saith the Lord of Hosts." (Zechariah 4:6 KJV). "And I will pray the Father, and He shall give you another comforter, that He may abide with you forever; Even the Spirit of truth whom the world cannot receive, because it seeth Him not, neither know Him; for He dwelleth in you, and shall be in you." (John 14:16, 17 KJV).**

Our performance and achievement level for Christ is consistent with our vision. "Conquerors for Christ" control their vision and change it as they are directed by the Holy Spirit, by activating their violent faith, thereby fulfilling their prophetic destiny as "change agents" for Christ Jesus. The most effective way to assure success and significance in the eyes of Almighty God is to diligently engage a proactive and dynamic goal oriented process to effect your vision. **"The plan of the diligent lead to profit as sure as haste leads to poverty." (Proverbs 21:5 KJV).** Commit to and do the plan to turn your vision into goals and your goals into reality! By first devising your goals, pursuant to your vision, and then taking action on your goals, you demonstrate the power of passion and purpose — the power of the Holy Spirit — in your day by day pursuit of excellence in Christ Jesus. Praise the Lord! **"Not as though I had already attained, either were already perfect: but I follow after, if that I may apprehend that for which also I am apprehended of Christ Jesus. Brethren, I count myself not to have apprehended: but this one thing I do, forgetting those things which are behind, and reaching forth unto those things which are before, I press toward the mark for the prize of the high calling of God in Christ Jesus." (Philippians 3:12-14 KJV). "...According to your faith be it done unto you." (Matthew 9:29 KJV). "[T]he Kingdom of Heaven suffereth violence, and the violent take it by force." Matthew 11:12 KJV). "But we all, with open face beholding as in a glass the glory of the Lord, are changed into the same image from glory to glory, evan as by the Spirit of the Lord." (2 Corinthians3:18 KJV). "...Go ye into all the world, and preach the Gospel to every creature." (Mark 16:15 KJV).**

    The sequence of this process is to first establish a vision, by the power of the Holy Ghost, and reduce the same to writing by creating a vision statement, which is the formal expression of your vision. Next, identify all of the barriers and obstacles, which stand in your way and are blocking you from achieving your vision. You should be able to identify as many as 20-25 separate barriers — and it is crucial that you be as honest as you can be with yourself. Now you need to prioritize these barriers and select the top five (5) that you feel are the most onerous in this regard. You then take each of the top five (5) negative, debilitating barriers and transform them into positive, declarative, empowering, present tense, first person action statements. Be certain that you use present tense action verbs such as, (by the power of the Holy Spirit) I can, have, do, sense, experience, am, demonstrate, activate etc., so that you actually experience the victory in your subconscious mind, as well as in your spirit, before you realize the same in your conscious mind. As you achieve your goals, seek the wisdom of the Holy Spirit to write new empowered and anointed goals, by the power of the Holy Spirit, which shall further advance your vision, and the kingdom of God on this earth! We are in the last of the last days and unto those who are diligent in their pursuit of Jesus Christ shall manifest all the power of the Godhead, with signs, wonders and miracles evident, for His honor and glory! Hallelujah! **"And be not conformed to this world: but be ye transformed by the renewing of your mind, that ye may prove what is that good, and acceptable, and perfect, will of God." (Romans 12:2 KJV).** **"Howbeit when He, the Spirit of truth, is come, He will guide you into all truth; for He shall not speak of Himself, but whatsoever He shall hear, that shall He speak; and He will show you things to come." (John 16:13 KJV).** **"And it shall come to pass in the last days, saith God, I will pour our of My Spirit upon all flesh: and your sons and your daughters shall prophesy, and your young men shall see visions, and your old men shall dream dreams...And I will show wonders in Heaven above, and signs in the earth beneath...And it shall come to pass, that whosoever shall call on the Name of the Lord shall be saved." (Acts 2:17, 19, 21 KJV).**

You see, we become what captures us. When Christ Jesus captures our hearts, we become overcomers in Christ to execute His perfect will, thus enforcing His victory over the adversary and all of the purveyors of evil. "Conquerors for Christ" accomplish this by asserting the power of Almighty God via the preaching of the Gospel of Christ Jesus — Christ crucified and the power of the Resurrection — with signs, wonders and miracles following. Therefore, we profit the Kingdom of God on this earth by winning souls to His Son, our Lord and Savior Jesus Christ! **"Thus saith the Lord, the Redeemer, the Holy One of Israel; I am the Lord thy God which teacheth thee to profit, which leadeth thee by the way thou shouldest go." (Isaiah 48:17 KJV).** "But we preach

Christ crucified...Christ the power of God, and the wisdom of God." (1 Corinthians 1:23, 14 KJV). "And now, Lord, behold their threatenings: and grant unto Thy servants, that with all boldness they may speak Thy Word, By stretching forth Thine hand to heal; and that signs and wonders may be done by the Name of Thy Holy Child Jesus. And when they had prayed, the place was shaken where they were assembled together, and they were all filled with the Holy Ghost, and they spake the Word of God with boldness...And with great power gave the apostles witness of the Resurrection of the Lord Jesus: and great grace was upon them all." (Acts 4:29-31, 33 KJV). "For whatsoever is born of God overcometh the world: and this is the victory that overcometh the world, even our faith. Who is he that overcometh the world, but he that believeth that Jesus is the Son of God." (1 John 5:4, 5 KJV).

Let us choose to fully activate our violent faith and be the "Conquerors for Christ" that Almighty God has chosen us to be by responding to Abba Father's clarion call to His chosen kings and priests in the marketplace and beyond, in our daily lives. Let us be single minded and consummately focused on our vision — our passion and purpose — to be overcomers for Jesus Christ on this earth, and to make a significant difference by making provision for Almighty God's vision by devising and then executing our vision and goals on a daily basis! Let us pursue "Our Vision & Goals" in Jesus' mighty Name, thereby filling the earth with the knowledge of the glory of the Lord — with the Gospel of Jesus Christ! Hallelujah!. Amen. "And the Lord answered me, and said, Write the vision, and make it plain upon the tables, that he may run that readeth it." (Habakkuk 2:2 KJV). "Looking unto Jesus the Author and Finisher of our faith; who for the joy that was set before Him endured the cross, despising the shame, and is set down at the right hand of the throne of God." (Hebrews 12:2 KJV). "For the earth shall be filled with the knowledge of the glory of the Lord, as the waters cover the sea." (Habakkuk 2:14 KJV). "Nay, in all these things we are more than conquerors through Him that loved us." (Romans 8:37 KJV).

"But they that wait upon the Lord shall renew their strength; they shall mount up with wings as eagles; they shall run, and not be weary; and they shall walk, and not faint." (Isaiah 40:31 KJV).

Discipline to Disciple — Terms of Discipleship

"Jesus saith unto them; "My meat is to do the will of Him that sent me, and to finish His work." (John 4:34 KJV).

In the previous message we addressed vision, goals, and being successful and significant in the eyes of Almighty God. We explored goal writing techniques and how to transform disempowering barriers (which prevent us from fulfilling our vision) into empowering action statements (which enable us to fulfill our vision). I trust that you have reflected upon your vision with the Holy Spirit and have undertaken and accomplished the worthy exercise of goal writing. Let there be no mistake, this is the condition precedent to achieving your vision in the marketplace and beyond, in your daily lives, thus being successful and significant in the eyes of Almighty God as His chosen kings and priests. **"Where there is no vision the people perish." (Proverbs 29:18 KJV). "And the Lord answered me, and said, Write the vision, and make it plain upon the tables, that he may run that readeth it."(Habakkuk 2:2 KJV).**

Let us focus on the requisite discipline of body, mind (soul) and spirit we must embody and demonstrate to achieve the goals we have devised, which will make our vision a reality. We must be specific in our goals and remain consummately focused on the objective at hand! **"And every man that striveth for the mastery is temperate in all things. Now they do it to obtain a corruptible crown; but we an incorruptible. I therefore so run, not as uncertainly: so fight I not as one that beateth the air: But I keep under my body, and bring it under subjection: lest that by any means,** when I have preached to others, I myself should be a castaway." (1 Corinthians 9:25-27 KJV. We must pay the price to be victorious and triumphant overcomers for Jesus Christ by constantly and diligently building up our faith through preparation, patience and perseverance in the face of continual attack, persecution, slander and the like, from a relentless adversary. We must be trained up in the discipline of a Soldier of the Cross of Jesus Christ so that we are empowered to enforce His victory against said adversary at every turn! We must endure and overcome affliction and hardness to become the mighty evangelists and witnesses that Christ has chosen us to be - - the mighty "Conquerors for Christ"! Hallelujah! **"Knowing this, that the trying of your faith worketh patience. But let patience have her perfect work, that ye may be perfect and entire, wanting nothing." (James 1:3, 4 KJV). "Thou therefore, my son, be strong in the grace that is in Christ Jesus...Thou therefore endure hardness as a good soldier of Jesus Christ." (2 Timothy 2:1, 2 KJV). "But watch thou in all things, endure afflictions, do the work of an evangelist, make full proof of thy ministry." (2 Timothy 4:5 KJV).**

The threshold attitude to develop is the mental and spiritual discipline of Christ Jesus. **"...But we have the mind of Christ." (1 Corinthians 2:16 KJV). "Let this mind be in you , which was also in Christ Jesus." (Philippians 2:5 KJV).** We need to achieve our goals mentally and spiritually, before the same shall be realized in the natural. In other words, we must envision the excellence of Christ Jesus in us, by the power of the Holy Spirit. For example, before evangelizing, witnessing, preaching or teaching the Word of God, we need to take the necessary time in study and meditation of the Word of God, and invest the requisite time in prayer with the Holy Spirit, which shall ensure that we are properly prepared, prayed up and focused on the mission at hand. We must yield to the Holy Spirit and be directed exclusively by His counsel and wisdom in all ministry, so that we flow in His mighty anointing and power! Remember that two of the primary reasons the Spirit of Truth is dwelling in the saved of Christ on this earth is to testify of Christ, and to glorify Christ, through you and me, the "Conquerors for Christ"! All Glory to God! **"Study to show thyself approved** unto God, a workman that needeth not to be ashamed, rightly dividing the Word of truth." (2 Timothy 2:15 KJV). **"And the Spirit of the Lord shall rest upon Him, the Spirit of wisdom and understanding, the Spirit of counsel and might, the Spirit of knowledge and of fear of the Lord."** (Isaiah 11:2 KJV). **"But the Comforter, which is the Holy Ghost, whom the Father will send in My Name, He shall teach you all things, and bring all things to your remembrance, whatsoever I have said unto you."** (John 14:26 KJV). **"But when the Comforter is come, whom I will send unto you from the Father, even the Spirit of truth, which proceedeth from the Father, He shall testify of Me."** (John 15:26 KJV). **"Howbeit when He, the Spirit of truth, is come, He will guide you into all truth: for He shall not speak of Himself; but whatsoever He shall hear, that shall He speak: and He will show you things to come. He shall glorify Me: for He shall receive of Mine, and shall show it unto you."** (John 16:13, 14 KJV).

The word disciple derives from the word discipline. To be a disciple of Christ Jesus we must be disciplined in His Word and by the power of the Holy Spirit. We must demonstrate and live His attitude, mind and Spirit! The terms of discipleship in Christ, which are written in Holy Scripture, reveal those who are truly his disciples, as well as those who are frauds, false preachers, false prophets, false teachers, heretics and hypocrites. True disciples bear the fruit of the Spirit, which is the character of Christ Jesus, because this is Father God's purpose for us on this earth. Frauds bear the fruit of the adversary, which fruit is contaminated, corrupt and rotten. **"But the fruit of the Spirit is love, joy, peace, long-suffering, gentleness, goodness, faith, Meekness, temperance: against such there is no law."** (Galatians 5:22, 23 KJV). **"For whom He did foreknow, He also did predestinate to be conformed to the image of his Son..."** (Romans 8:29 KJV). **"Beware of false prophets, which come to you in sheep's clothing, but inwardly they are ravening wolves. Ye shall know them by their fruits...Every tree that bringeth not forth good fruit is hewn down, and cast into the fire. Wherefore by their fruits ye shall know them. Not every one that saith unto Me, Lord, Lord, shall enter into the Kingdom of Heaven; but he that doeth the will of My Father which is in Heaven. Many** will say to Me in that day, Lord, Lord, have we not prophesied in Thy Name? and in Thy Name have cast out devils? and in Thy Name done many wonderful works? And then will I profess unto them, I never knew you: depart from Me, ye that work iniquity." (Matthew 7:15-23 KJV).

Submission and obedience to Christ Jesus and to His Word are the fundamental requirements of discipleship, from which all others flow. Christ is our perfect example of submission and obedience unto Father God. Jesus Christ was obedient unto death, even the death of the cross. Jesus Christ is the epitome of humility and contriteness, which are the conditions precedent to submission and obedience. He emptied Himself of His glory, though not of His deity, to become lowly man, in order to become sin for you and me. He became man to die a substitutionary death for us on the cross. He demonstrated for us the sacrificial love of the Father, Son and Holy Ghost. He commands the same of His disciples. This sacrificial love is unconditional and unmerited for the unworthy and undeserving sinners of the world to come to the Cross of Christ and receive eternal salvation. This is unfailing love, which always seeks the highest good of others. It is love by choice and will - - it is love by faith! Hallelujah! **"For I have given you an example, that ye should do as I have done to you."** (John 13:15 KJV). **"And being found in fashion as a man, He humbled Himself, and became obedient unto death, even the death of the cross."** (Philippians 2:8 KJV). **"For even here unto were ye called: because Christ also suffered for us, leaving us an example, that we should follow His steps..."** (1 Peter 2:21 KJV). **"If ye love Me, keep My commandments."** (John 14:15 KJV). **"He that hath My commandments, and keepeth them, he it is that loveth Me: and he that loveth Me shall be loved of My Father, and I will love him, and will manifest Myself to him.** (John 14:21 KJV). **"...If a man love Me, he will keep My Words: and My Father will love him, and We will come unto him, and make Our abode with him."** (John 14:23 KJV). **"God is love."** (1 John 4:8, 16 KJV). **"For God so loved the world, that He gave His only begotten Son, that whosoever believeth in Him should not perish, but have everlasting life."** (John 3:16 KJV). **"Hereby perceive we the love of God, because He laid down His life for us: and we ought to lay down our lives for the brethren." (1 John 3:16 KJV). "Greater love hath no man than this, that a man lay down his life for his friends." (John 15:13 KJV). "For the love of Christ constraineth us...that they which live should not henceforth live unto themselves, but unto Him which died for them and rose again." (2 Corinthians 5:14, 15 KJV). "...[T]he love of God is shed abroad in our hearts by the Holy Ghost which is given unto us." (Romans 5:5 KJV).

One of the elements of the fruit of the Spirit is "faith" (Galatians 5:22, 23 KJV), which is interpreted as "faithfulness". Faithfulness becomes another term of discipleship. Are we faithful to Christ Jesus and the "Great Commission" by evangelizing lost souls (fruit) to His Kingdom? Are we faithful executors, stewards and trustees of the faith, and of the Gospel of Jesus Christ, by contending for the faith and by defending and confirming the Gospel? Can Jesus Christ, our Commander-in-Chief, depend on us to assert the power of Almighty God against the enemy, thereby enforcing the victory of His Cross and Resurrection? **"I am the vine, ye are the branches: He that abideth in Me, and I in him, the same bringeth forth much fruit: for without Me ye can do nothing...Herein is My Father glorified, that ye bear much fruit; so shall ye be My disciples." (John 15:5, 8 KJV). "According to the glorious Gospel of the blessed God, which was committed to my trust." (1 Timothy 1:11 KJV). "O Timothy, keep that which is committed to thy trust..." (1 Timothy 6:20 KJV). "...[I]n the defense and confirmation of the Gospel...I am set for the defense of the Gospel..." (Philippians 1:7, 17 KJV). "Beloved, when I gave all diligence to write unto you of the common salvation, it was needful for me to write unto you, and exhort you that ye should earnestly contend for the faith..." (Jude 1:3 KJV). "For the preaching of the cross...is the power of God." (1 Corinthians 1:18 KJV).**

Steadfastness is another term of discipleship. Steadfastness is maintaining determination, perseverance and persistence, at all cost, in one's endeavors for Christ. **"Therefore, my beloved brethren, be ye steadfast, unmovable, always abounding in the work of the Lord..." (1 Corinthians 15:58 KJV).** We continue in our relentless pursuit of Christ Jesus and His Word, and hold on to our freedom in Him and our confidence in the faith, while resisting our formidable enemy, enduring chastisement for personal growth into Christ, bearing persecution and slander for preaching His Gospel and defending Christian liberty, at every turn. Steadfastness involves one's discipline to establish a goal and then to effectively run the race of faith to attain said goal, which is Christ Jesus! We enforce Christ's victory withstanding the onslaughts of the enemy, having done all to stand, thus advancing Christ's line of conquest around the world! We never give up! All glory to God! Hallelujah! "...If ye continue in My Word, then are ye My disciples indeed; and ye shall know the truth, and the truth shall make you free. If the Son therefore shall make you free, ye shall be free indeed." (John 8:31, 32, 36 KJV). "...[Y]et am I with you in the spirit, joying and beholding your order, and the steadfastness of your faith in Christ." (Colossians 2:5 KJV). "But Christ as a Son over his own house; whose house are we, if we hold fast the confidence and the rejoicing of the hope firm unto the end. For we are made partakers of Christ if we hold the beginning of our confidence steadfast unto the end." (Hebrews 3:6, 14 KJV). "Be sober, be vigilant; because your adversary the devil, as a roaring lion, walketh about, seeking whom he may devour: Whom resist steadfast in the faith, knowing that the same afflictions are accomplished in your brethren that are in the world." (1 Peter 5:8, 9 KJV). "For whom the Lord loveth He chasteneth, and scourgeth every son whom He receiveth. If ye endure chastening, God dealeth with you as with sons; for what son is he that the father chasteneth not." (Hebrews 12:6, 7 KJV). "And ye shall be hated of all men for My Name's sake: but he that endureth to the end shall be saved." (Matthew 10:22 KJV). "Who shall separate us from the love of Christ? shall tribulation, or distress, or persecution, or famine, or nakedness, or peril, or sword?...Nay, in all these things we are more than conquerors through Him that loved us." (Romans 8:35, 37 KJV). "Stand fast therefore in the liberty wherewith Christ hath made us free, and be not entangled again with the yoke of bondage." (Galatians 5:1 KJV). "I press toward the mark for the prize of the high calling of God in Christ Jesus." (Philippians

3:14 KJV). "...[L]et us run with patience the race that is set before us, Looking unto Jesus the Author and Finisher of our faith; who for the joy that was set before Him endured the cross despising the shame, and is set down at the right hand of the throne of God." (Hebrews 12:1, 2 KJV). "Wherefore take unto you the whole armor of God, that ye may be able to withstand in the evil day, and having done all, to stand." (Ephesians 6:13 KJV). "To him that overcometh will I grant to sit with Me in My throne, even as I also overcame, and am set down with My Father in His throne." (Revelation 3:21 KJV).

The terms of discipleship also include the surrender of all — all of who we are — all of what we have, unto Christ Jesus. Christ gave His ALL for us on the cross, and He commands the same of His disciples. Jesus Christ is The King of kings and the Lord of lords, our Prophet, Priest and King, our Lord and Savior, the Captain of the Hosts of Heaven (our Commander-in-Chief), the Lamb of God, the Perfect Sacrifice, the Alpha and Omega, the Author and Finisher of our faith, The Word of God, The Son of God, God the Son, and more. And He commands that we die to self, pride, the enemy, sin, sin nature, the ways of the world, death, sickness, oppression and possession of demons, and take up His Cross daily, and follow Him, thereby enforcing His victory of the Cross and the power of His Resurrection! Therefore, as we, the "Conquerors for Christ", execute our "Great Commission", we are fulfilling Father God's purpose for us on this earth by being changed into the same character and image as our Lord and Savior Jesus Christ! By the power of the Holy Spirit, we have the authority and power to say and execute with Jesus Christ, "**...My meat is to do the will of Him that sent Me, and to finish His work.**" (John 4:34 KJV). All Glory to God! Praise You Lord Jesus! "**If any man come to me, and hate not his father, and mother, and wife, and children, and brethren, and sisters, yea, and his own life also, he cannot be My disciple... So likewise, whosoever he be of you that foresaketh not all that he hath, he cannot be My disciple.**" (Luke 14:26, 33 KJV). "**If any man will come after Me, let him deny himself, and take up his cross daily, and follow Me.**" Luke 9:23 KJV). "**And he that taketh not his cross, and followeth after Me, is not worthy of**

Me." (Matthew 10:38 KJV). "And whosoever doth not bear his cross, and come after Me, cannot be My disciple."(Luke 14:27 KJV).

"But they that wait upon the Lord shall renew their strength; they shall mount up with wings as eagles; they shall run, and not be weary; and they shall walk, and not faint." (Isaiah 40:31 KJV).

Loyalty, Unity, Esprit de Corps

As we pursue excellence in Christ being our sovereign God's kings and priests, it is imperative that we actively seek and receive the Gifts of the Holy Spirit, which gifts manifest the power of Jesus Christ against the enemy. The battle we engage is one of the heart, soul and spirit — the battle to assert the power of Almighty God against the adversary, sin, false preachers, prophets and teachers in the apostate church, and the ways of the world. In order that we prosper and succeed in this quest, we must overcome the multitude of humanistic, materialistic and secular temptations with which we are confronted. The more we bear the fruit of the Spirit, which is the character of Christ, the more the Holy Spirit of the living God shall pour forth from our bellies as rivers of living water, in blessings, victory and resurrection life. The gifts of the Holy Spirit are manifested to edify — to build up — the body of Christ, as well as, to astonish and astound a lost and dying world! **"But the manifestation of the Spirit is given to every man to profit withal. For to one is given by the Spirit the word of wisdom; to another the word of knowledge by the same Spirit; To another faith by the same Spirit; to another the gifts of healing by the same Spirit; To another the working of miracles; to another prophecy; to another discerning of spirits; to another divers kinds of tongues; to another the interpretation of tongues: But all these worketh that one and the selfsame Spirit, dividing severally as He will." (1 Corinthians 12:7-11 KJV).** "And the Spirit of the Lord shall rest **upon him, the Spirit of wisdom and understanding, the Spirit of council and might, the Spirit of knowledge and of fear of the Lord." (Isaiah 11:2 KJV). "But the fruit of the Spirit is love, joy,** peace, longsuffering, gentleness, faith, meekness, temperance: against such there is no law." (Galatians 5:22,23 KJV). "He that believeth on Me, as the scripture hath said, out of his belly shall flow rivers of living water." (John 7:38 KJV).

Pursuing excellence is an acquired attribute — it is an attitudinal decision of the heart, soul and spirit — and is fueled by the power of the Holy Spirit, who empowers us to activate our violent faith to the end. The greatest gift God has given us is His only begotten Son, Jesus Christ the Righteous, who is the perfect example after whom to pattern our pursuit of excellence. We all agree that leadership by example is the most effective leadership style, and God has blessed us by having Jesus Christ provide us The WAY to enforce His victory! PRAISE GOD! "...[T]he Kingdom suffereth violence, and the violent take it by force." (Matthew 11:12 KJV). "For I have given you an example, that ye should do as I have done to you." (John 13:15 KJV). "For even hereunto were ye called because Christ also suffered for us, leaving us an example, that ye should follow His steps. (1 Peter 2:21 KJV). "Let this mind be in you, which was also in Christ Jesus." (Philippians 2:5 KJV).

Our purpose on this earth is to be changed into the character and image of Jesus Christ. Being a disciple of Jesus Christ means exemplifying Him in everything that we say, do and think — to have the very discipline of the mind of Christ Jesus — what better mentor and roll model could there be? When we follow the example of Jesus Christ, we are readily assured that we shall not succumb to Satan's pleasures by cavorting with those who would be purveyors of wickedness, hate, anger, duplicity and deceit. "Make no friendship with an angry man; and with a furious man thou shalt not go: Lest thou learn his ways, and get a snare to thy soul." (Proverbs 22:24,25 KJV). "A wise man feareth, and departeth from evil: but the fool rageth, and is confident. He that is soon angry dealeth foolishly: and a man of wicked devices is hated (Proverbs 14:16,17 KJV). "For whom He did foreknow, He also did predestinate to be conformed to the image of His Son..." (Romans 8:29 KJV). "But whosoever doth not bear his cross, and come after Me, cannot be My disciple." (Luke 14:27 KJV). "...But we have the mind of Christ." (1 Corinthians 2:16 KJV).

The enemy's strategy is to divide and conquer the church of Jesus Christ. Therefore, it behooves us to be eternally vigilant to guard our vision, principles and oneness before God. **"Let all bitterness, and wrath, and anger, and clamor, and evil speaking be put away from you, with all malice: And be ye kind to one another, tenderhearted, forgiving one another, even as God for Christ's sake hath forgiven you." (Ephesians 4:31,32 KJV). "Be sober, be vigilant; because your adversary the devil, as a roaring lion, walketh about, seeking whom he may devour." (1 Peter 5:8 KJV).**

Fellow "Conquerors for Christ", beware of those among us who would clandestinely seek to subvert and destroy our God-given opportunity for Christ Jesus in the marketplace and beyond, in our daily lives. Allow no man, woman or child the power to undo the Body of Christ from without or within by sowing discord via pride, lies, slander, gossip, jealousy, backbiting, false witness, hate, anger, and the like. If any of us discovers, or become privy to, any such efforts, we must place our leaders on notice so that we may successfully manage the situation and eradicate the evil with all dispatch — for a house divided against itself cannot stand! **"And Jesus knew their thoughts, and said unto them, every kingdom divided against itself is brought to desolation: and every city or house divided against itself shall not stand." (Matthew 12:25 KJV). "These six things doth the Lord hate: yea, seven are an abomination unto Him: a proud look, a lying tongue, and hands that shed innocent blood, A heart that deviseth wicked imaginations, feet that be swift in running to mischief, A false witness that speaketh lies, and he that soweth discord among the brethren." (Proverbs 6:16, 17 KJV).**

We have been chosen by our God and Father to be His kings and priests on this earth — to be the servant leaders, stewards and ministers of His marketplace and beyond, in our daily lives. How privileged we are! PRAISE YOU, ABBA, FATHER! In the marketplace, as well as in the church, both Almighty God's creations, the Holy Spirit has orchestrated an intricate system in which we pursue our passion and purpose for Jesus Christ. Within this system — His Kingdom Authority — we are responsible to perform specific roles.

It is incumbent upon us to acknowledge our role, embrace the same, and then fulfill said role with all the due diligence we are able to muster, in the most positive, proactive fashion possible. **"That there should be no schism in the body; but that the members should have the same care one for another...Now ye are the body of Christ, and members in particular. And God hath set some in the church..."** (1 Corinthians 12:25, 27, 28 KJV). **"Let a man so account of us, as the ministers of Christ, and stewards of the mysteries of God. Moreover, it is required in stewards, that a man be found faithful."** (1 Corinthians 4:1,2 KJV). Moreover, we must respect and honor one another as "Conquerors for Christ" and as fellow Christian brothers and sisters. There is no room for dissension, parochialism, self-centeredness or negativity. These are the diabolical ways of Satan, the antichrist, and the purveyors of evil. The WAY of Jesus Christ involves loyalty, pluralism, esprit de corps and positive "CAN DO" action! I remind you that the literal interpretation of king is — "CAN DO"! **"Obey them that have rule over you, and submit yourselves..."** (Hebrews 13:17 KJV). **"Submitting yourselves one to another in the fear of God."** (Ephesians 5:21 KJV). **"I can do all things through Christ which strengtheneth me."** (Philippians 4:13 KJV).

Colleagues in Christ, we must be one Body in Christ. We are called to oneness in and with the Holy Trinity. Esprit de corps means "the spirit of the body" It is the common spirit existing in the members of a group. We are the Body of Christ — His kingdom on earth, joined together and duly purchased by His precious blood. Furthermore, as His chosen kings and priests in the marketplace and beyond, in our daily lives, we are sanctified in a very select and special way to spread the Gospel of Jesus Christ via our grassroots evangelism and to the whole of the world. There is no more occasion to tarry! The time has come for us to execute our "Great Commission" as the Army of the Light! Let us come together in unity under the blood stained banner of the Cross of Jesus Christ! In the spirit of oneness, let us resolve and pledge, here and now, to fulfill our "Great Commission" — and truly BE the kings and priests He has chosen us to be — demonstrating "Loyalty, Unity and Esprit de Corps"! PRAISE YOU FATHER! **"Now I beseech you,** brethren, by the name of our Lord Jesus Christ, that ye all speak the same thing, and that there be no divisions among you; but that ye be perfectly joined together in the same mind and in the same judgment." (1 Corinthians 1:10 KJV). "...[T]hat ye stand fast in one Spirit, with one mind striving together for the faith of the Gospel." (Philippians 1:27 KJV). "Endeavoring to keep the unity of the Spirit in the bond of peace. There is one body, and one Spirit, even as ye are called in one hope of your calling; One Lord, one faith, one baptism, One God and Father of all, who is above all, and through all, and in you all." (Ephesians 4:3-6 KJV). "...[T]hat they may be one , as we are...That they all may be one; as Thou, Father, art in Me, and I in Thee, that they also may be one in Us, that the world may believe that Thou hast sent Me...[A]nd that the world may know that Thou hast sent Me, and hast loved them, as Thou hast loved ME." (John 17:11, 21, 23 KJV).

"But they that wait upon the Lord shall renew their strength; they shall mount up with wings as eagles; they shall run, and not be weary; and they shall walk, and not faint." (Isaiah 40:31 KJV).

Influence Our World and Enforce the Victory of Christ

"And this Gospel of the Kingdom shall be preached in all the world for a witness unto all nations; and then shall the end come." (Matthew 24:14 KJV).

As "Conquerors for Christ", our role in this prophetic scripture is significant, indeed. By the intricate, supernatural orchestration of the Holy Spirit, we have been commanded a most vital opportunity to influence and fulfill Almighty God's plan on this earth. "...**Not by might, nor by power, but by My Spirit, saith the Lord of hosts."** (Zechariah 4:6 KJV). We are to hold ourselves out as the evangelists and disciples of Jesus Christ, to influence, to grow, to build, to teach, to love and to nurture the body of Christ in the marketplace and beyond, in our daily lives. We are to influence our world and enforce the victory of the Cross of Christ and the power of His Resurrection, by bringing the lost and dying to the end of themselves, at the Cross of Christ. **"For the preaching of the cross is to them that perish foolishness; but unto us that are saved it is the power of God."** (1 Corinthians 18 KJV). We are in the holy and sanctified position to, and indeed, we are commanded to, influence our world for Christ Jesus, thereby advancing the "Great Commission" by actively demonstrating our violent faith to the world."...**[T]he Kingdom of Heaven suffereth violence, and the violent take it by force."** (Matthew 11:12 KJV). As Christ Jesus is the light of the world, so are we, as His joint-heirs. Therefore, we are commanded to influence our world by shining forth the glory of God that is in us! Yes, His very presence (glory) lives in us by the indwelling and infilling of the Holy Ghost! We influence our world by boldly and passionately living and proclaiming Jesus Christ and His Gospel! **"And if children, then heirs of God, and joint-heirs with Christ..." (Romans 8:17 KJV). "Then spake Jesus again unto them, saying, I am the light of the world: he that followeth Me shall not walk in darkness, but shall have the light of life." (John 8:12 KJV). "Ye are the light of the world. A city that is set on a hill cannot be hid. Let your light so shine before men, that they may see your good works, and glorify your Father which is in heaven." (Matthew 5:14, 16 KJV).**

Our sovereign God authorizes our activity! Our "Great Commission" is from Him! Truly, He commands that we **"...Go ye into all the world, and preach the Gospel to every creature." (Mark 16:15 KJV).** Almighty God gives us all the authority necessary in Holy Scripture. When we stand on His Word, we have nothing to fear! When we speak His Word, we have nothing to fear! When we demonstrate His Word, we have nothing to fear! **"And when they had prayed, the place was shaken where they were assembled together; and they were all filled with the Holy Ghost, and they spake the word of God with boldness." (Acts 5:31 KJV). "For God hath not given us the spirit of fear; but of power, and of love, and of a sound mind." (2 Timothy 1:7 KJV). "...Fear not: believe only..." (Luke 8:50 KJV). "...Fear not; I am the first and the last: I am He that liveth, and was dead; and, behold, I am alive for evermore, Amen; and have the keys of hell and of death." (Revelation 1:17, 18 KJV).** Let us be confident, forceful, daring and fearless — yes — let us be bold for Jesus! Praise God! **"And for me, that utterance may be given unto me, that I may open my mouth boldly, to make known the mystery of the Gospel, For which I am an ambassador in bonds: that therein I may speak boldly, as I ought to speak." (Ephesians 6:19, 20 KJV).**

We have been granted all the appropriate and necessary blessings, gifts, grace and weapons of Almighty God to influence the world and enforce the victory of our Lord and Savior Jesus Christ over the enemy!

We are armed with the Name of Jesus, which is the Name above all names, at whose Name the adversary and all of his demons tremble in fear and flee! When we pray, minister and engage spiritual warfare, we proclaim the Word of God, in the Name of Jesus Christ our Lord, which means that we assert the power of God against the enemy based on the finished work of the Cross of Jesus Christ! Hallelujah! **"But then He answered and said, It is written, Man shall not live by bread alone, but by every word that proceedeth out of the mouth of God."** (Matthew 4:4 KJV). **"Jesus said unto him, It is written again, Thou shalt not tempt the Lord Thy God."** (Matthew 4:7 KJV). **"Then Jesus saith unto him, Get the hence, Satan: for it is written, Thou shalt worship the Lord Thy God, and Him only shalt thou serve.** (Matthew 4:10 KJV). **"When Jesus therefore had received the vinegar, He said, It is finished..."** (John 19:32 KJV). **"And having spoiled principalities and powers, He made a show of them openly, triumphing over them in it."** (Colossians 2:15 KJV). **"Wherefore God also hath highly exalted Him, and given Him a Name which is above every Name: That at the Name of Jesus every knee should bow... And that every tongue should confess that Jesus Christ is Lord, to the glory of God the Father."** (Philippians 2:9-11 KJV).

We are armed with the blood of Christ Jesus! Nothing evil can penetrate the blood! We are overcomers by the blood of the Lamb! We overcome the adversary and all of his demons! We overcome sin, sin nature, death, all illness, sickness, infirmity, oppression and possession of demons! Glory to God! The blood of Jesus redeems us, forgives us, cleanses us, justifies us, sanctifies us, and glorifies us! Hallelujah! **"And they overcame him by the blood of the Lamb, and by the word of their testimony..."** (Revelation 12:11 KJV). **"In whom we have redemption through His blood, the forgiveness of sins, according to the riches of His grace..."** (Ephesians 1:7 KJV). **"But if we walk in the light, as He is in the light, we have fellowship one with another, and the blood of Jesus cleanses us from all sin."** (1 John 1:7 KJV). **"Much more then, being now justified in His blood, we shall be saved from wrath through Him."** (Romans 5:9 KJV). **"Wherefore Jesus also, that He might sanctify the people with His own blood, suffered without the gate."** (Hebrews 13:12 KJV). **"...[A]nd whom He justified, them He also glorified."** (Romans 8:30 KJV).

We are armed with the Armor of God, the Armor of Light and the Armor of Righteousness! We are armed with the Lord Jesus Christ, who has won THE VICTORY for evermore! We actually put on the indestructible and eternally triumphant Lamb of God, the Lord of lords and King of kings! Hallelujah! **"Finally, my brethren, be strong in the Lord, and in the power of His might. Put on the whole armor of God, that ye may be able to stand against the wiles of the devil..."** (Ephesians 6:10-20 KJV). **"...[L]et us put on the armor of light."** (Romans 13:12 KJV). **"By the word of truth, by the power of God, by the armor of righteousness on the right hand and on the left."** (2 Corinthians 6:7 KJV). **"But put ye on the Lord Jesus Christ, and make not provision for the flesh, to fulfill the lusts thereof."** (Romans 13:14 KJV). **"These shall make war with the Lamb, and the Lamb shall overcome them: for He is Lord of lords, and King of kings: and they that are with Him are called, and chosen, and faithful."** (Revelation 17:14 KJV).

We are armed with prayer! Prayer is communicating with the Father, in the Name of Jesus Christ. Through prayer, we know the perfect will of the Father, as we hear from His Holy Spirit! When we pray with a pure heart, the Father engages all of His power on our behalf, so that we always enforce the victory of Christ Jesus! All Glory to God! **"Have faith in God. For verily I say unto you, That whosoever shall say unto this mountain, Be thou removed, and be thou cast into the sea; and shall not doubt in his heart, but shall believe that these things which he saith shall come to pass; he shall have whatsoever he saith. Therefore I say unto you, What things soever ye desire, when ye pray, believe that ye receive them, and ye shall have them. And when ye stand praying, forgive, if ye have aught against any: that your Father also which is in Heaven may forgive you your trespasses."** (Mark 11:22-25 KJV). **"Verily, verily, I say unto you, He that believeth on Me, the works that I do shall he do also; and greater works than these shall he do; because I go unto My Father. And whatsoever ye shall ask in My Name, that will I do, that the Father may be glorified in the Son. If ye ask anything in My Name, I will do it."** (John 14:12-14 KJV). **"...Verily, verily, I say unto you, Whatsoever ye shall ask the Father in My Name, He will give it you. Hitherto have ye asked nothing in My Name: ask, and ye shall receive, that your joy may be full." (John 16:23, 24 KJV).

We are armed with praise. Praise is directly connected with the Lord's intent to establish His Kingdom on this earth at his second coming. Therefore, when we praise Him, we are engaging and enforcing His power over the defeated adversary, while preparing the way for His Millennial Kingdom! Hallelujah! **"Let the high praises of God be in their mouth, and a twoedged sword in their hand; to execute vengeance upon the heathen, and punishments among the people; To bind their kings with chains, and their nobles with fetters of iron; To execute the judgment written: this honor have all the saints. Praise ye the Lord." (Psalm 146:6-9 KJV).**

We are armed with the weapon of preaching. It is by our preaching the Gospel of Christ Jesus that souls are brought to the Cross of Christ and convicted of their sin. The preaching of the Word of God is the power of God unto repentance, forgiveness and salvation! Preaching the truth defeats the enemy at every turn! Praise the Lord! **"For the preaching of the cross...is the power of God." (1 Corinthians 1:18 KJV). "For I am not ashamed of the Gospel of Christ: for it is the power of God unto salvation to everyone that believeth..." (Romans 1:16 KJV). "So shall My Word be that goeth forth out of My mouth: it shall not return unto Me void, but it shall accomplish that which I please, and it shall prosper in the thing whereto I sent it." (Isaiah 55:11 KJV). "For the Word of God is quick, and powerful, and sharper than any twoedged sword, piercing even to the dividing asunder of soul and spirit, and of the joints and marrow, and is a discerner of the thoughts and intents of the heart." (Hebrews 4:12 KJV).**

We are armed with our testimony. We are to testify as to what the Word of God has done for us. Our testimony overcomes the adversary, while witnessing to, and thus preparing, lost and dying souls to come to Christ Jesus! Hallelujah! **"And I heard a loud voice in Heaven, Now is come salvation, and strength, and the Kingdom of our God, and the power of His Christ: for the accuser of our brethren is cast down, which accused them before our God day and night. And they overcame him by the blood of the Lamb,** and by the Word of their testimony; and they loved not their lives to the death." (Revelation 12:10, 11 KJV).

We are armed with the weapon of the gifts of the Holy Spirit. Our responsibility as "Conquerors for Christ" is to assert the power of Almighty God against the devil, sin, death, sin nature, sickness, oppression and possession of demons, the false preachers, prophets and teachers in the church, as well as, the ways of the world. Our Almighty Father accomplishes this by releasing His power through the kings and priests of Jesus Christ, by manifesting signs, wonders and miracles by the power and gifts of the Holy Ghost. We are to persevere in continuing to seek Almighty God's Kingdom and all of His righteousness, hungering and thirsting for Christ's presence and power! We do this by activating our violent faith, thereby yielding to His Holy Spirit, and allowing Him to flow forth from our bellies as rivers of living water in blessings, victory and resurrection life! All Glory to God! **"Behold, I give unto you power to tread on serpents, and scorpions, and over all the power of the enemy: and nothing shall by any means hurt you." (Luke 10:19 KJV). "But seek ye first the Kingdom of God, and His righteousness; and all these things shall be added unto you." (Matthew 6:33 KJV). "...[T]he Kingdom of Heaven suffereth violence, and the violent take it by force." (Matthew 11:12 KJV). "For to one is given by the Spirit the word of wisdom; to another the word of knowledge by the same Spirit; To another faith by the same Spirit; to another the gifts of healing by the same Spirit; To another the working of miracles; to another prophecy; to another discerning of spirits; to another diverse tongues; to another the interpretation of tongues..." (1 Corinthians 12:8-10 KJV).**

Fellow "Conquerors for Christ", let us faithfully influence our world and enforce the victory of Christ, by vigorously executing the battle plan of our Commander-in-Chief! Let us be the positive influences of Christ and His Gospel in our world by being His examples unto a lost and dying world! **"So that ye were examples to all that believe...For from you sounded out the Word of the Lord... in every place your faith to God-ward is spread abroad..." (1 Thessalonians 1:7, 8 KJV). "That ye may be blameless and harmless, the sons of God, without rebuke, in the midst of a** crooked and perverse nation, among whom ye shine as lights in the world: Holding forth the Word of life..." (Philippians 2:15, 16 KJV). "...[T]he love of God is shed abroad in our hearts by the Holy Ghost which is given unto us." (Romans 5:5 KJV). O "Conquerors for Christ", let us ensure that "[T]his Gospel of the Kingdom shall be preached in all the world for a witness unto all nations; and then shall the end come." (Matthew 24:14 KJV).

Soldiers of the Cross of Christ Jesus, let us soar as the eagles in Almighty God's Heavenlies, as we "Influence Our World and Enforce the Victory of Christ!" "But thanks be to God, which giveth us the victory through our Lord Jesus Christ." (1 Corinthians 15:57 KJV).

> "But they that wait upon the Lord shall renew their strength; they shall mount up with wings as eagles; they shall run, and not be weary; and they shall walk, and not faint." (Isaiah 40:31 KJV).

Leadership — Showing "The Way"

Our Lord and Savior Jesus Christ offers "The Way" to Heaven, as well as, "The Way" of Leadership by example here on earth. Our success and significance on this earth in the eyes of Almighty God depend upon our faithful obedience in following the perfect example of the Son of God! We must yield ourselves unto the Spirit of God in favor of Christ Jesus! **"I am the way, the truth and the life: no man cometh unto the Father, but by Me." (John 14:6 KJV). "Good and upright is the Lord: therefore will He teach sinners in the way. The meek He will guide in judgment: and the meek He will teach His way." (Psalm 24:8, 9 KJV). "If you love Me, keep My commandments." (John 14:15 KJV). "If a man love Me, he will keep My words: and My Father will love him, and We will come unto him, and make our abode with him." (John 14:23 KJV). "...Behold, to obey is better than sacrifice, and to hearken than the fat of rams." (1 Samuel 15:22 KJV). "For I have given you an example, that ye should do as I have done unto you." (John 13:15 KJV). "For even hereunto were called: because Christ also suffered for us, leaving us an example, that ye should follow in His steps." (1 Peter 2:21 KJV). "Teach me Thy Way, O Lord, and lead me in the plain path, because of mine enemies." (Psalm 27:11 KJV)**

Leadership in Christ is showing "The Way" with great diligence; to stand in front; to direct, guide and lead by the power of the Holy Ghost. Christ appoints the leadership of the church, which is known as the Five-Fold Ministry. It consists of the offices of Apostles, Prophets, Evangelists, Pastors and Teachers. However, whoever is called and chosen by Christ is to be a leader unto Him, while submitting and obeying Kingdom Authority through the Five-Fold Ministry. Therefore, leadership in Christ is to influence and persuade others by boldly preaching and teaching the Gospel of Jesus Christ, as well as, demonstrating and witnessing Christ in our daily lives. When we lead by the example of Christ, we esteem and love our Lord and Savior with all that we are — with everything in our being — with all that we can muster! We yield to the Holy Spirit of the living God and take care to put forth constant and careful effort, in diligent study, to be disciplined, edified and trained up in the Word of God. We then persevere in the quest to recruit, discipline, edify and train up other "Conquerors for Christ" in the Army of the Light by diligently preaching, teaching, demonstrating and witnessing the Gospel of Jesus Christ. Thus, we pursue the very essence and virtue of Christ Jesus. We are being changed into His very character and image, which is Father God's divine purpose for each of us! Praise God! **"For Thou art my Rock and my Fortress; therefore for Thy Name's sake lead me and guide me." (Psalm 31:3 KJV) "Lead me to the Rock that is higher than I." (Psalm 61:2 KJV). "I will instruct thee and teach thee in 'the way' which thou shalt go: I will guide thee with Mine eye." (Psalm 32:8 KJV). "Keep thy heart with all diligence; for out of it are the issues of life." (Proverbs 4:23 KJV). "Wherefore, beloved, seeing that ye look for such things, be diligent that ye may be found of Him in peace, without spot, and blameless." (2 Peter 3:14 KJV). "For the love of Christ constraineth us; because we thus judge, that if one died for all, then were all dead: And that He died for all, that they which live should not henceforth live unto themselves, but unto Him which died for them, and rose again." (2 Corinthians 5:14, 15 KJV). "Study to show thyself approved unto God, a workman that needeth not to be ashamed, rightly dividing the Word of truth." (2 Timothy 2:15 KJV). "All scripture is given by inspiration of God, and is profitable for doctrine, for reproof, for correction, for instruction in righteousness: That the man of God may be perfect, thoroughly furnished unto all good works." (2 Timothy 3:16, 17 KJV). "Finally, brethren, whatsoever things are true, whatsoever things are honest, whatsoever things are just, whatsoever things are pure, whatsoever things are lovely,** whatsoever things are of good report; if there be any virtue, and if there be any praise, think on these things. Those things, which ye have both learned, and received, and heard, and seen in me, do; and the God of peace shall be with you." (Philippians 4:8, 9 KJV). "Put on therefore, as the elect of God, holy and beloved, bowels of mercies, kindness, humbleness of mind, meekness, long-suffering; Forbearing one another, and forgiving one another, if any man have a quarrel with any: even as Christ forgave you, so also do ye. And above all these things put on charity, which is the bond of perfectness. And let the peace of God rule in your hearts, to the which also ye are called in one body; and be ye thankful. Let the Word of Christ dwell in you richly in all wisdom; teaching and admonishing one another in psalms and hymns and spiritual songs, singing with grace in your hearts to the Lord. And whatsoever ye do in word or deed, do all in the Name of the Lord Jesus, giving thanks to God and the Father by Him." (Colossians 3:12-17.KJV). "Grace and peace be multiplied unto you through the knowledge of God, and of Jesus Christ our Lord. According as His divine power hath given unto us all things that pertain unto life and godliness, through the knowledge of Him that hath called us to glory and virtue: Whereby are given unto us exceeding great and precious promises: that by these ye might be partakers of the divine nature, having escaped the corruption that is in the world through lust. And beside this, giving all diligence, add to your faith virtue; and to virtue knowledge; And to knowledge temperance; and to temperance patience; and to patience godliness; And to godliness brotherly kindness; and to brotherly kindness charity. For if these things be in you, and abound, they make you that ye shall neither be barren nor unfruitful in the knowledge of our Lord Jesus Christ. But he that lacketh these things is blind, and cannot see afar off, and hath forgotten that he was purged from his old sins. Wherefore the rather, brethren, give diligence to make your calling and election sure: for if ye do these things, ye shall never fall." (2 Peter 1:2-10 KJV). "And He gave some, apostles; and some, prophets; and some, evangelists; and some, pastors and teachers; For the perfecting of the saints, for the work of the ministry, for the edifying of the body of Christ: Till we all come in the unity of the faith, and the knowledge of the Son of God, unto a perfect man, unto the measure of the stature of the fullness of Christ." (Ephesians 4:11-13 KJV). "And He said unto them, Go ye into all the world, and preach the Gospel to every creature." (Mark 16:15 KJV).

Bearing the fruit of the Spirit, which is the character of Jesus Christ, who the greatest leader in all of history, is our goal. Disciple comes from the word discipline — we are disciplined in the very Mind, Spirit and Word of Christ! Remember that Christ is the Word made flesh. He is the perfect manifestation and revelation of the Father. Being His disciple means exemplifying Him in everything we say, do and think — what better Role Model could there be? As we seek first the Kingdom of God, who is Christ Jesus, and His righteousness, who is Christ Jesus, then all of the power and authority of Father God, Christ Jesus and the Holy Ghost manifest through us! Hallelujah! This is "The Way" we work out our own salvation and, by yielding to the Holy Spirit, enable Father God to work in us His divine will. My prayer is that we purpose to pursue Christ Jesus and are endued with the grace and power of the Holy Spirit so that we actively demonstrate and live Jesus Christ — that we are of the same Mind — and one with Him in Spirit! Thus, we shall be "Conquerors for Christ" and overcomers for Him on this earth by showing our fellow men, women and children "The Way" to salvation through His shed blood on the cross, as well as, "The Way" unto sanctification and holiness in His character. **"But the fruit of the Spirit is love, joy, peace, long-suffering, gentleness, goodness, faith, Meekness, temperance: against such there is no law." (Galatians 5: 22, 23 KJV). "And He saith unto them, Follow Me, and I will make you fishers of men." (Matthew 4:19 KJV). "And the Word was made flesh, and dwelt among us, (and we beheld His glory, the glory as of the only begotten of the Father,) Full of grace and truth." (John 1:14 KJV). "For whom He did foreknow, He also did predestinate to be conformed to the image of His Son..." (Romans 8:29 KJV). "But we all, with open face beholding as in a glass the glory of the Lord, are changed into the same image from glory to glory, even as by the Spirit of the**

Lord." (2 Corinthians 3:18 KJV). "If ye continue in My Word, then ye are My disciples indeed; And ye shall know the truth, and the truth shall make you free." (John 9:31,32 KJV). "But seek ye first the Kingdom of God, and His righteousness; and all these things shall be added unto you." (Matthew 6:33 KJV). "...[W]ork out your own salvation with fear and trembling. For it is God which worketh in you both to will and to do of His good pleasure." (Philippians 2:12, 13 KJV). "Let this mind be in you, which was also in Christ Jesus..." (Philippians 2:5 KJV). "And he that overcometh and keepeth My works unto the end, to him will I give power over the nations." (Revelation 2:26 KJV).

The leadership of Jesus Christ involves the notion of servant-leadership. The more we pursue being changed into the character and image of Christ Jesus — the more we bear His fruit — the more we come to understand that the hallmark virtues of the Kingdom of God are humility, contriteness, sacrificial love and obedience. We esteem others higher than ourselves. We continually die to self, pride, sin, sin nature, the enemy and the ways of the world, in favor of demonstrating the Resurrection life and power of Jesus Christ. We know that without Christ we are nothing, but with Him all things are possible. We live a life of repentance and realize that it is the love of Christ that constrains us to obey His "Great Commission"! This is "The Way" we are able to valiantly continue the preaching, teaching, demonstration and witness of Christ and Him crucified and the power of His Resurrection, in the face of false witness, slander and all manner of evil and lies, as propagated against us by the adversary and his cohorts. When we remain focused on Jesus Christ, we are people of the Holy Spirit and hence, are able to rise above all of these assaults, thus asserting all of the power of the Father against the enemy, thereby enforcing Christ's victory through His Cross and Resurrection. We are the chosen leaders of the Kingdom of God — of Christ's Army of the Light — of the body of Christ — of the ecclesia, the called out ones — of the church of Jesus Christ! We are highly chosen to demonstrate "Leadership — Showing "The Way" as the "Conquerors for Christ"! Amen and Hallelujah! "...**If any man desire to be first, the same shall be last of all, and servant of all." (Luke 9:33 KJV).** "And there was also a strife among them, which of them should be accounted the greatest. And He said to them, The kings of the Gentiles exercise lordship over them; and they that exercise authority upon them are called benefactors. But ye shall not be so: but he that is greatest among you, let him be the younger; and he that is chief, as he that doth serve. For whether is greater, he that sitteth at meat, or he that serveth? is not he that sitteth at meat? but I am among you as He that serveth. Ye are they which have continued with Me in My temptations. And I appoint unto you a Kingdom, as My Father has appointed unto Me; that ye may eat and drink at My table in My Kingdom, and sit on thrones judging the twelve tribes of Israel." (Luke 22:24-30 KJV). "If I then, your Lord and Master, have washed your feet; ye also ought to wash one another's feet. For I have given you an example, that ye should do as I have done to you. Verily, verily, I say unto you, The servant is not greater than his lord; neither he that is sent greater than he that sent him." (John 13:14-16 KJV). "Let this mind be in you, which was also in Christ Jesus: Who, being in the form of God... made Himself of no reputation, and took upon Him the form of a servant, and was made in the likeness of men: And being found in fashion as a man, He humbled Himself, and became obedient unto death, even the death of the cross. Wherefore God also hath highly exalted Him, and given Him a Name which is above every name: That at the Name of Jesus every Knee should bow...And that every tongue should confess that Jesus Christ is Lord, to the glory of God the Father." (Philippians 2:5-11 KJV). "Looking unto Jesus the Author and Finisher of our faith; who for the joy that was set before Him endured the cross despising the shame, and is set down at the right hand of the throne of God." (Hebrews 12:2 KJV). "For even hereunto were ye called: because Christ also suffered for us, leaving us an example, that ye should follow His steps: WHO DID NO SIN, NEITHER WAS GUILE FOUND IN HIS MOUTH: Who, when He was reviled, reviled not again; when He suffered, He threatened not; but committed Himself to Him that judgeth righteously: Who His own self bare our sins in His own body on the tree, that we, being dead to sins, should live unto righteousness: BY WHOSE

STRIPES YE WERE HEALED." (1 Peter 2:21-24 KJV). "And hast made us unto our God kings and priests: and we shall reign on the earth." (Revelation 5:10 KJV). "Nay, in all these things we are more than conquerors through Him that loved us." (Romans 8:37 KJV). "But thanks be to God, which giveth us the victory through our Lord Jesus Christ." (1 Corinthians 15:57 KJV).

"But they that wait upon the Lord shall renew their strength; they shall mount up with wings as eagles; they shall run, and not be weary; and they shall walk, and not faint." (Isaiah 40:31 KJV).

Faithful Stewardship

Stewardship is to hold something in trust for another. It involves the notion of faithfully and properly administering and managing the resources of another. For example, an executor of another's last will and testament, and/or the trustee of another's estate, constitute a stewardship relationship. This stewardship relationship holds one to the highest of standards and responsibility, because the executor, steward, and/or trustee, is legally and morally bound to act in the best interests of, and execute strictly, the desires of the testator. In the experience of our personal relationship with Jesus Christ, we are the executors, stewards and trustees of the last will and testament (His Gospel and Great Commission) of the testator, who is our Lord and Savior Jesus Christ. Thus, we are held to the highest of standards and responsibility by Christ Jesus, Himself, to faithfully and properly execute His Gospel and Great Commission! Hallelujah! I am certain you agree, that there exists no greater nor higher honor, than to fulfill the duties of "Faithful Stewardship" on behalf of the King of kings and Lord of lords! Indeed, the government of the church is upon our shoulders as the kings and priests of Jesus Christ, to contend for, defend and confirm the faith and Gospel of our Lord and Savior Jesus Christ! All Glory to God! **"For unto us a child is born, unto us a Son is given: and the government shall be upon His shoulder...Of the increase of His government and peace, there shall be no end...The zeal of the Lord of Hosts shall perform this." (Isaiah 9:6, 7 KJV). "According to the glorious Gospel of the blessed God, which was committed to my trust." (1 Timothy 1:11 KJV). "O Timothy, keep that which is committed to thy trust..." (1 Timothy 6:20 KJV). "...[W]oe is** unto me if I preach not the Gospel." (1 Corinthians 9:16 KJV). "...[A]nd in the defense and confirmation of the Gospel, ye are partakers of my grace." (Philippians 1:7 KJV). "...[K]nowing that I am set for the defense of the Gospel." (Philippians 1:17 KJV). "Beloved, when I gave all diligence to write unto you of the common salvation, it was needful for me to write unto you, and exhort you that ye should earnestly contend for the faith which was once delivered unto the saints." (Jude 3 KJV).

In our personal relationship with Christ Jesus, "Faithful Stewardship" also contemplates our service to others with the primary commitment to the larger community, in lieu of our own self-interest. In our secular culture, we face the pressures of self-interest, or parochialism, on a daily basis. Our society has become a misguided community based upon entitlement, which is bondage (self-centered) as opposed to freedom and liberty in Christ, which is pluralism (other-centered), and with this phenomenon, we have lost the true meaning and sense of community. All we care about is ourselves, and largely give no thought of the welfare of others. This becomes the responsibility of the government. Our Sovereign God has chosen us to be His stewards by serving our fellow men, women and children, pursuant to the perfect example of His Son Jesus Christ. His commands are entirely antithetical to the reality in our world today. Each day we must die to self and our pride and take up the Cross of Christ, thereby summoning the moral courage, by the power of the Holy Ghost, to choose to be the servant leaders of Jesus Christ, and execute our "Faithful Stewardship" as ministers of Almighty God's blessings, gifts and grace, for the good of our fellow men, women and children. **"But he that is greatest among you shall be your servant."** (Matthew 23:11 KJV). "For I have given you an example, that ye should do as I have done to you." (John 13:15 HJV). "And He said to them all, If any man will come after Me, let Him deny Himself, and take up His cross daily, and follow Me." (Luke 9:23 KJV). "But God forbid that I should glory, save in the cross of our Lord Jesus Christ, by whom the world is crucified unto me, and I unto the world. (Galatians 6:14 KJV). "As every man hath received the gift, even so minister the same one to another, as good stewards of the manifold grace of God. **If any man speak, let him speak as the oracles of God; if any man minister, let him do it as of the ability which God giveth: that God in all things may be glorified through Jesus Christ, to whom be praise and dominion for ever and ever. Amen."** (1 Peter 4:10-11 KJV).

The antidote and cure to self-interest is to commit to a cause — something outside of ourselves — a cause for which we have so much passion that we willingly endure the sacrifice, risk and adventure which is attendant to the commitment. Indeed, there are many causes in the world today — many of which are nothing more than mis-guided efforts at self-aggrandizement and self-exaltation. Jesus Christ is our Lord and Savior. I submit unto you that it is our relationship with the person of Jesus Christ — Christ and Him crucified and the power of the Resurrection — that is the only legitimate and true cause for mankind. Almighty God has chosen us to be His kings and priests to rescue lost souls for Jesus Christ and to enforce His Victory in the marketplace and beyond, in our daily lives, as His "Conquerors for Christ"! Is there anything that is more compelling, or more crucial to the course of humanity, than to be "Faithful Stewards" committed unto the person of Jesus Christ? **"And hath made us kings and priests unto God and His Father; to Him be glory and dominion for ever and ever. Amen"** (Revelation 1:6 KJV). **"And hath made us unto our God kings and priests: and we shall reign on the earth."** (Revelation 5:10 KJV). Do you see that through Jesus, we have freedom from self-interest? **"And ye shall know the truth, and the truth shall make you free."** (John 8:32 KJV). **"If the Son therefore shall make you free, ye shall be free indeed."** (John 8:36 KJV). **"Stand fast in the liberty wherewith Christ hath made us free, and be not entangled again with the yoke of bondage."** (Galatians 5:1 KJV). Do you understand that by demonstrating Jesus' example we are serving Father God and our fellow men, women and children? Do you know that by activating our violent faith and integrity in Christ, we are Almighty God's "Faithful Stewards"? Can you appreciate that the person of Jesus Christ and the truth of His Gospel is the only cause worthy of your commitment? God has blessed us with the holy and sanctified platform from which to be His oracles and ministers -- to be His

"Faithful Stewards"! Shall we be deemed worthy when we meet our Lord and Savior? "...[T]he **Kingdom of Heaven suffereth violence, and the violent take it by force." (Matthew 11:12 KJV). "For I am not ashamed of the Gospel of Christ: for it is the power of God unto salvation to every one that believeth..." (Romans 1:16 KJV). "Let a man so account of us, as of the ministers of Christ, and stewards of the mysteries of God. Moreover, it is required in stewards, that a man be found faithful. For I know nothing by myself; yet am I not hereby justified: but He that judgeth me is the Lord." (1 Corinthians 4: 1-2, 4 KJV).**

We are morally responsible and accountable for the discretionary deployment and use of Almighty God's resources with respect to the needs of Jesus Christ's Kingdom and Community on this earth. Almighty God's resources include the Gospel of Jesus Christ, provision for the vision, our time on this earth, and our God-given skills, talents and opportunities, as the Holy Spirit presents us as divine appointments for Christ Jesus. It is incumbent upon us, through Christ, to boldly create the requisite passion and commitment to execute our defining prophetic purpose and destiny. We are His chosen kings and priests and our cause for Christ is to make provision for His vision and preach the Gospel of our Lord and Savior Jesus Christ to all nations. Our battlefield and platform is the marketplace and beyond, in our daily lives. Let us diligently and shrewdly, by the power of the Holy Spirit, apply our respective God-given abilities to advance the Kingdom of Christ, for the glory of God and the honor of Jesus Christ! Let us faithfully engage and demonstrate our "Faithful Stewardship", and hence, fulfill our prophetic destiny, which is Christ Jesus' bold trust in each of us! **"And Jesus came and spake unto them, saying, All power is given unto Me in Heaven and in earth. Go ye therefore, and teach all nations, baptizing them in the Name of the Father, and of the Son, and of the Holy Ghost: Teaching them to observe all things whatsoever I have commanded you: and, lo, I am with you always, even unto the end of the world. Amen. (Matthew 28:18-20 KJV). "And whatsoever ye do, do it heartily, as to the Lord, and not unto men; Knowing that of the Lord ye shall** receive the reward of inheritance: for ye serve the Lord Christ. (Colossians 3:23-24 KJV).

"But they that wait upon the Lord shall renew their strength; they shall mount up with wings as eagles; they shall run, and not be weary; and they shall walk, and not faint." (Isaiah 40:31 KJV).

Passion — The Fire of the Holy Ghost

Let us reflect and meditate with the Holy Spirit on the word passion. Passion creates compelling and intense enthusiasm for action toward a given goal, purpose, or relationship. Passion causes an unrelenting love and desire toward said goal, purpose, or relationship which, when activated, enables an overcoming and overpowering effect. Passion stirs up the eagerness to pursue a cause with courageous, vigorous, untiring activity and zeal. Applied to our cause as Christ's kings and priests in the marketplace and beyond, in our daily lives, passion is the fire of the Holy Ghost! The fire of the Holy Ghost creates compelling and intense enthusiasm for our action to be changed into the image of Christ Jesus. The fire of the Holy Ghost causes our unrelenting love and desire toward Almighty God, Jesus Christ and the Holy Spirit, and stirs up the gifts of God in us, which enable us to courageously and vigorously assert the power of Almighty God against the adversary and enforce the Victory of Christ's Cross and Resurrection daily, with great zeal! The fire of the Holy Ghost activates our violent faith to demonstrate our passion in our Sovereign Father, Jesus Christ and the Holy Spirit, in the execution of our "Great Commission". Hallelujah! **"...He shall baptize you with the Holy Ghost, and with fire." (Matthew 3:11; Luke 3:16 KJV). "Watch ye, stand fast in the faith, quit you like men, be strong." (1 Corinthians 16:13 KJV). "Be ye of good courage, and He shall strengthen your heart, all ye that hope in the Lord." (Psalm 31:24 KJV). "Now the Lord is that Spirit: and where the Spirit of the Lord is, there is liberty. But we all, with open face beholding as in a glass the glory of the Lord, are changed into the same image from glory to glory, even as** by the Spirit of the Lord." (2 Corinthians 3:17, 18 KJV). "For the love of Christ constraineth us; because we thus judge, that if one died for all, then all were dead: And that He died for all, that they which live should not live unto themselves, but unto Him which died for them, and rose again." (2 Corinthians 5:14, 15 KJV). "Wherefore I put thee in rembrance that thou stir up the gift of God which is in thee by the putting on of my hands." (2 Timothy 1:6 KJV). "Of the increase of His government and peace there shall be no end...The zeal of the Lord of Hosts will perform this." (Isaiah 6:7 KJV). "Behold, I give you power to tread on serpents and scorpions, and over all the power of the enemy: and nothing shall by any means hurt you." (Luke 10:19 KJV). "For the preaching of the cross...is the power of God." (1 Corinthians 1:18 KJV). "...[T]he Kingdom of Heaven suffereth violence, and the violent take it by force." (Matthew 11:12 KJV). "...Go ye into all the world, and preach the Gospel to every creature." (Mark 16:15 KJV).

"Conquerors for Christ" are highly chosen to pursue the noble and virtuous work of evangelism and discipleship for justice and righteousness, and join Christ Jesus in recreating the world via our witness of Him. It is the realization of this holy and sanctified vision and Cause for Christ that ignites the fire and passion for our lives, through the power of the Holy Spirit. As we pursue our passion of being "change agents" for Jesus Christ, we discover that we are being changed and transformed into peacemakers — pure in heart — and more Christ-like each day. We are bearing the fruit of the Spirit! We are being conformed to the image of Christ Jesus, which is the Father's purpose for each of us! We are highly chosen to be co-laborers with Almighty God as we work to make His Kingdom on earth visible and real, as it is in Heaven, by sharing the Gospel of Jesus Christ with the world. Passionately and daily, with the fire of the Holy Ghost, we deny ourselves and take up the blood stained banner of the Cross of Christ, and follow Him! Hallelujah! "Go ye therefore, and teach all nations, baptizing them in the name of the Father, and of the Son, and of the Holy Ghost." (Matthew 28:19 KJV). "Go ye into all the world, and preach the Gospel to every creature." (Mark 16:15 KJV). "And they overcame him by the blood of the Lamb, and by the Word of their testimony; and they loved not their lives unto the death." (Revelation 12:11 KJV). "But ye shall receive power, after that the Holy Ghost is come upon you: and ye shall be witnesses unto Me in both Jerusalem, and in all Judea, and in Samaria, and unto the uttermost part of the earth." (Acts 1:8 KJV). "For whom He did foreknow, He also did predestinate to be conformed to the image of His Son..." (Romans 8:29 KJV). "But the fruit of the Spirit is love, joy, peace, long-suffering, gentleness, goodness, faith, Meekness, temperance: against such there is no law." (Galatians 5:22, 23 KJV). "For we are laborers together with God..." (1 Corinthians 3:9 KJV). "If any man will come after Me, let him deny himself, and take up his cross daily, and follow Me." (Luke 9:23 KJV). "And he that taketh not his cross, and followeth after Me, is not worthy of Me." (Matthew 10:38 KJV). "And whosoever doth not bear his cross, and come after Me, cannot be My disciple." (Luke 14:27 KJV).

Almighty God never said that our fulfilling of His vision for us would be easy. Indeed, each of us is responsible and accountable to Him to work out our own salvation as we do that which He has chosen us to do. "... **[W]ork out your own salvation with fear and trembling. For it is God which worketh in you both to will and to do of His good pleasure.**" (Philippians 2:12,13 KJV). God the Creator — has created us — to be creative, by the power of the Comforter, who is the Holy Spirit of Truth, in order to accomplish our mission on this earth. **"But when the Comforter is come, whom I will send unto you from the Father, even the Spirit of truth, which proceedeth from the Father, He shall testify of Me."** (John 15:26 KJV). **"Howbeit when He, the Spirit of truth is come, He will guide you into all truth:...and He will show you things to come...He shall glorify Me..."** (John 16:13, 14 KJV). He has chosen us to execute and to live out the dreams and visions with which He has blessed us. He has chosen us to dare to step out in faith and truth, thereby securing the great and awesome things He has commanded us to do. Do we exhibit the vigorous passion and active, violent faith to live our lives according to His vision? **"Where there is no vision the people perish: but he that keepeth the law, happy** is he." (Proverbs 29:18 KJV). "To open their eyes, and to turn them from darkness to light, and from the power of Satan unto God, that they may receive forgiveness of sins, and inheritance among them which are sanctified by faith that is in Me." (Acts 26:18 KJV).

I know we all agree that passionate action for Jesus Christ — demonstrating our ultimate love for Him in everything we do and are — is The Way to be. Therefore, let us eschew the ruts of procrastination, indecisiveness, lack of courage and the lack of will to try, so that the opportunity for victory shall not escape our grasp. Let us choose to fully activate our violent faith and demonstrate our passionate love for Almighty God by answering His clarion call to His chosen kings and priests. Let us have the "Passion — The Fire of the Holy Ghost" for Jesus Christ, by being consummately focused on our vision and thus, live the passion to seize our opportunity to be overcomers for Christ and enforcers of His Victory in the marketplace and beyond, in our daily lives! **"Finally, my brethren, be strong in the Lord, and in the power of His might." (Ephesians 6:10 KJV). "For whatsoever is born of God overcometh the world: and this is the victory that overcometh the world, even our faith. Who is he that overcometh the world, but he that believeth that Jesus Christ is the Son of God?" (1 John 5:4,5 KJV).**

May God endue us with the power, the fire, and the brilliance of the Holy Spirit so that we may "Soar as the Eagles" in His Heavenlies and advance the "Great Commission" with the complete and overcoming passion of a prophet! **"And thou, child, shalt be called the prophet of the Highest: for thou shalt go before the face of the Lord to prepare His ways." (Luke 1:76 KJV). "...Not by might, nor by power, but by My Spirit, saith the Lord of Hosts." (Zechariah 4:6 KJV).**

> **"But they that wait upon the Lord shall renew their strength; they shall mount up with wings as eagles; they shall run, and not be weary; and they shall walk, and not faint." (Isaiah 40:31 KJV).**

Our Greatest Destiny & Highest Nobility

I respectfully invite you to prayerfully reflect and meditate on the following scripture verse: **"But they that wait upon the Lord shall renew their strength; they shall mount up with wings as eagles; they shall run, and not be weary; and they shall walk, and not faint."** (Isaiah 40:31 KJV).

The Lord God made you and me for Himself. He made us for relationship. It necessarily follows that He shall supply us with every need through His blessings, gifts and grace. He provides us with His salvation, strength, courage, and divine revelation through the saving blood of Jesus Christ, Holy Scripture and the infilling of the Holy Spirit. He provides us with the victory of the Cross and the power of the Resurrection of Jesus Christ! **"I am the way, the truth and the life: no man cometh unto the Father, but by Me."** (John 14:6 KJV). **"And the Spirit of the Lord shall rest upon him, the Spirit of wisdom and understanding, the Spirit of counsel and might, the Spirit of knowledge and of fear of the Lord."** (Isaiah 11:2 KJV). **"But we preach Christ crucified...Christ, the power of God and the wisdom of God."** (1 Corinthians 1:23, 24 KJV).

Our sovereign Father has a divine purpose — a prophetic destiny — for each of us to fulfill. He has blessed us with a great and most challenging opportunity — one by which we are to pursue the noble and virtuous work of being "change agents" for Jesus by advancing the "Great Commission" from the grassroots of our commerce centers and throughout the world. We have been chosen to do this as we stand against the formidable power of a very strong enemy — the devil. Who among us is not at times weary and ready to faint? Who among us does not require God's awesome love, glory and power to inspire us with new strength and courage? Are we confident in His deliverance? Do we actively know and believe that He will never disappoint us? Do we demonstrate through our active, violent faith and integrity, the confident assurance, bold hope and joyful expectation in His promise? Do we live in courage and stand fast in strength to wait upon the Lord? **"Let integrity and uprightness preserve me; for I wait on Thee." (Psalm 25:21 KJV). "Wait on the Lord: be of good courage, and He shall strengthen thine heart: wait, I say, on the Lord." (Psalm 27:14 KJV). "And this is the confidence that we have in Him, that, if we ask anything according to His will, He heareth us: And if we know that He hear us, whatsoever we ask, we know that we have the petitions that we desired of Him." (1 John 5:14, 15 KJV).**

God promises that those who wait upon Him shall never be ashamed. We never wait in vain. We win! Our patience and service honors Him greatly because it is our highest expression of faith! We actively consent to be in the hands of God! Could we experience a higher blessing? **"Yea, let none that wait on Thee be ashamed:" (Psalm 25:3 KJV). "Rest in the Lord, and wait patiently for Him: fret not thyself because of him that prospereth in his way... For evildoers shall be cut off: but those that wait upon the Lord, they shall inherit the earth." (Psalm 37:7,9 KJV). "Come unto Me, all ye that labor and are heavy laden, and I will give you rest. Take My yoke upon you, and learn from Me; for I am meek and lowly in heart: and ye shall find rest unto your souls. For My yoke is easy, and My burden is light." (Matthew 11:28-30 KJV).**

We must wait on God in fervent prayer and service. The more time we spend in His presence, the greater He blesses us with the revelation of His ways. Do we fervently pray to Father God about our divine opportunity to serve Him in the marketplace and beyond, in our daily lives? When we wait and pray, we are like the eagle. Prayer gives us the ability to mount up and soar majestically in the ways of the Holy Spirit. Just as the eagle spreads its wings and soars upward when the currents are right, we, as Almighty God's kings and priests — His "Conquerors for Christ" — spread our wings and soar in the ways of His Word. We soar in His will, with His strength and omnipotence, on His wings — His Way! We run and do not get weary. We walk and do not faint. Why? Because we are one with Him — and God never gets weary — nor does He faint. Our God is the Everlasting and Almighty One — The great I AM THAT I AM! Let us highly resolve that we shall obey our Lord God, Abba Father and fulfill His purpose for us on this earth — to be conformed and changed into the image of His Son Jesus Christ! Praise God through Jesus Christ, our Lord and Savior! As we are changed into the image of Christ Jesus, we bear His fruit and manifest His authority and power! We are constrained by His love in us to do His work! This is the answer to our prayers! This is our prophetic destiny! Hallelujah! **"The effectual fervent prayer of a righteous man availeth much." (James 5:16 KJV). "And all things, whatsoever ye shall ask in prayer, believing, ye shall receive." (Matthew 21:22 KJV). "And we know that all things work together for good to them that love God, to them who are called according to His purpose. For whom He did foreknow, He also did predestinate to be conformed to the image of His Son, that He might be the first-born among many brethren." (Romans 8:28, 29 KJV). "Now the Lord is that Spirit: and where the Spirit of the Lord is, there is liberty. But we all, with open face beholding as in a glass the glory of the Lord, are changed into the same image from glory to glory, even as by the Spirit of the lord." (2 Corinthians 3:17, 18 KJV). "For the love of Christ constraineth us...[T]hat they which live should not live unto themselves, but unto Him which died for them, and rose again." (2 Corinthians 5:14, 15 KJV).**

Let us choose to faithfully execute our "Great Commission", which Almighty God has bestowed upon us. Let us wait for, and on Him, through prayer and service, thereby being changed into the character and image of Jesus Christ His Son, thus fulfilling "Our Greatest Destiny and Highest Nobility"! Then we shall be overcomers for Jesus Christ and enforcers of His Victory! All glory to God! **"For whatsoever is born of God overcometh the world: and this is the victory that overcometh the world, even our faith. Who is he that overcometh the world, but he that believeth that Jesus is the Son of God." (1 John 5:4, 5 KJV). "And hast made** us unto our God kings and priests: and we shall reign on the earth." (Revelation 5:10 KJV).

"But they that wait upon the Lord shall renew their strength; they shall mount up with wings as eagles; they shall run, and not be weary; and they shall walk, and not faint." (Isaiah 40:31 KJV).

Our Most Significant Responsibility

"And Jesus came and spoke unto them, saying, All power is given unto Me in heaven and in earth. Go ye therefore, and teach all nations, baptizing them in the name of the Father, and of the Son, and of the Holy Ghost: Teaching them to observe all things whatsoever I have commanded you: and, lo, I am with you always, even unto the end of the world. Amen." (Matthew 28: 18-20 KJV).

Our "Great Commission" from the Lamb of God, Jesus Christ the Righteous, is so compelling! The question becomes whether we, as His "Conquerors for Christ", duly purchased by the blood of the Lamb of God, are responsible to our "Great Commission" from Jesus Christ. Being responsible is to assume and perform one's duties and obligations — to be accountable for one's actions and behavior to an authority who delegates said duties and obligations. Our authority emanates from, and is, Almighty God, through Jesus Christ, His Gospel and the indwelling and infilling of the Holy Ghost. Abba, Father created us with the freedom and ability to choose how we would be. He gave us the ability, through the power of the Holy Spirit, to change, grow, adapt, and be transformed into the image of Christ, thereby rising above our circumstances, while responding effectively to our changing world. Indeed, Abba Daddy has purposed that we are changed into the character of Christ Jesus from glory to glory, even as by the Spirit of the Lord! He has called us through the preaching of the Gospel. He has justified us and made us righteous by the holy and precious blood of His Son. He has glorified us by the indwelling and infilling presence of His Holy

Spirit. This is all possible due to the Cross of Christ and the power of His Resurrection. Christ Jesus has fulfilled His responsibility to you and me. Pray tell, what of our responsibility to Him? **"And be not conformed to this world: but be ye transformed by the renewing of your mind, that ye may prove what is that good, and acceptable, and perfect, will of God." (Romans 12:2 KJV).** "And we know that all things work together for good to them that love God, to them who are called according to His purpose. For whom He did foreknow, Hew also did predestinate to be conformed to the image of His Son, that He might be the first-born of many brethren. Moreover whom He did predestinate, them He also called: and whom He called, them He also justified: and whom He justified, them He also glorified." (Romans 8;28-30 KJV). "Now the Lord is that Spirit: and where the Spirit of the is, there is liberty. But we all, with open face beholding as in a glass the glory of the Lord, are changed into the same image from glory to glory, even as by the Spirit of the Lord." (2 Corinthians 3:17, 18 KJV). "And hath raised us up together, and made us sit together in heavenly places in Christ Jesus." (Ephesians 2:6 KJV). "But we preach Christ crucified...Christ the power of God, and the wisdom of God." (1 Corinthians 1;23, 24 KJV).

Being responsible involves taking effective and appropriate action to further our cause, our faith, our shared vision — our "Great Commission". How do we measure up to our responsibility as the kings and priests of Jesus Christ and as His overcomers on this earth? Let us prayerfully reflect upon our most significant responsibility. Are we actively pursuing all of the blessings, gifts, grace and supernatural weapons with which God has bestowed upon us and armed us? Are we demonstrating active, violent faith each and every day of our lives by executing our authority and power in Christ Jesus? Are we passionately evangelizing the Lamb of God, with the fire of the Holy Ghost, from the grassroots of our neighborhoods and around the world via the marketplace and the Internet? Are we proclaiming the Gospel with the love and fervor of a disciple of Christ Jesus? Are we consummately focused and dedicated to being the kings and priests that God has chosen us to be and making provision for His glorious vision? Are we exemplifying our Lord Jesus and advancing our "Great Commission" with every means God has provided us? Do we honor Christ Jesus and continually radiate His glory through our persistent and persevering action? Are we responsible to our personal love and relationship with Jesus Christ? Do we exalt Jesus Christ in all things? Have we recommitted to the authority of the Word of God? Are we enforcing the victory of the Cross of Christ and the power of His Resurrection, daily? Are we responsible to our "Great Commission"? **"(For the weapons of our warfare are not carnal, but mighty through God to the pulling down of strongholds;) Casting down imaginations, and every high thing that exalts itself against the knowledge of God, and bringing into captivity every thought to the obedience of Christ..." (2 Corinthians 10:4, 5 KJV). "...[T]he Kingdom of Heaven suffereth violence, and the violent take it by force." (Matthew 11:12 KJV). "And I say also unto thee, that thou art Peter, and upon this Rock I will build My church; and the gates of hell shall not prevail against it. And I will give unto thee the keys of the Kingdom of Heaven: and whatsoever thou shalt bind on earth shall be bound in Heaven: and whatsoever thou shalt loose on earth shall be loosed in Heaven." (Matthew 16:18, 19 KJV). "Behold, I give unto you power to tread on serpents and scorpions, and over all the power of the enemy: and nothing shall by any means hurt you." (Luke 10:19 KJV). "...Go ye into all the world, and preach the Gospel to every creature." (Mark 16:15 KJV). "And Jesus answered him, The first of all the commandments is, Hear, O Israel; the Lord our God is one Lord: And thou shalt love the Lord thy God with all thy heart, and with all thy soul, and with all thy mind, and with all thy strength: this is the first commandment. And the second is like, namely this, Thou shalt love thy neighbor as thyself. There is none other commandment greater than these." (Mark 12:29-31 KJV). "And He is the Head of the body, the church: who is the beginning, the first-born from the dead; that in all things He might have the pre-eminence." (Colossians 1:18 KJV). "For the ways of man are before the eyes of the Lord, and He pondereth all his goings." (Proverbs 5:21 KJV). "See then that ye walk circumspectly, not as fools, but as wise, redeeming the time, because the days are evil." (Ephesians 5:15,16 KJV).**

"No man, having put his hand to the plow, and looking back, is fit for the kingdom of God." (Luke 9:62 KJV).

Oh how blessed and highly chosen are we! Father God has given us the requisite authority and power we need to further our "Great Commission". We have the responsibility to choose to appropriate the same through the saving blood of the Lamb, the power of the Holy Spirit and the Gospel of Jesus Christ! Let us responsibly choose, NOW, to be "Conquerors for Christ", His overcomers and enforcers of His Victory! Let us responsibly choose to be His kings and priests of passion, purpose, integrity and active, violent faith, who stand on His truth, and having done all, to stand. Let us responsibly summon the moral courage and wherewithal, by the power of the Holy Spirit, to faithfully execute our holy, prophetic destiny to be evangelists and disciples of Jesus Christ in the marketplace and beyond, in our daily lives, hence fulfilling "Our Most Significant Responsibility" to the King of kings and Lord of lords! O Hallelujah! **"Ye have not chosen Me, but I have chosen you, and ordained you, that ye should go and bring forth fruit, and that your fruit should remain: that whatsoever ye shall ask of the Father in My Name, He may give it you." (John 15:16 KJV).** "That thou keep this commandment...until the appearing of our Lord Jesus Christ...[W]ho is the blessed and only potentate, the King of kings, and Lord of lords..." (1 Timothy 6:14, 15 KJV). "For whatsoever is born of God overcometh the world; and this is the victory that overcometh the world, even our faith. Who is He that overcometh the world, but he that believeth that Jesus is the Son of God?" (1 John 5:4,5 KJV). **"And hast made us unto our God kings and priests: and we shall reign on the earth." (Revelation 5:10 KJV.**

My fellow "Conquerors for Christ", you are ever present in our prayers and joyful expectation. We ask the same from you as we respectfully admonish and exhort one another and pursue the excellence of Christ Jesus, through the empowerment, wisdom and conviction of the Holy Spirit. **"And the Spirit of the Lord shall rest upon him, the Spirit of wisdom and understanding, the Spirit of counsel and might, the Spirit of knowledge and of fear of the Lord." (Isaiah 11:2 KJV).** "But ye shall receive power, after that the Holy Ghost is come upon you: and ye shall be witnesses unto Me both in Jerusalem, and in all Judea, and in Samaria, and unto the uttermost part of the earth." (Acts 1:8 KJV).

"But they that wait upon the Lord shall renew their strength; they shall mount up with wings as eagles; they shall run, and not be weary; and they shall walk, and not faint." (Isaiah 40:31 KJV).

More on Responsibility to Jesus

As Christians we are a free people. The precious blood of the Lamb of God has set us free. We are free to choose how we would be — how we would live — how we would respond (positive and empowering through the Holy Spirit) or react (negative and controlling of the devil thus sacrificing our freedom). If Jesus Christ has set us free in His Name and in His blood, then it becomes our responsibility to ACT responsibly toward our freedom. All too often we witness our responsibility as the forgotten side of our freedom. Why do people prefer being cared for by government? Why do people blame others for their "condition"? Why do people constantly complain yet remain complacent and inactive? Why do people shirk their duties and shrink from their responsibilities? Why do people blame others for their own lack of responsibility? Why do people lack the courage to ACT responsibly toward their freedom? Why is 97% of the population in the world today mediocre? Was Jesus mediocre? NAY, Jesus was and is the most empowered person to ever walk in this world! Does Jesus blame others for His "condition"? NEVER! Does Jesus complain yet remain inactive? NEVER! Does Jesus ever shirk His duties or shrink from His responsibilities? NEVER! He RESPONDS! Does Jesus fully exercise His freedom? ALWAYS! Do we? If not — WHY NOT? **"Stand fast therefore in the liberty wherewith Christ hath made us free, and be not entangled again with the yoke of bondage." (Galatians 5:1 KJV).** "And ye shall know the truth, and the truth shall make you free... If the Son therefore shall make you free, ye shall be free indeed." (John 8:32, 36 KJV). "But when the Comforter is come, whom I will send unto you from the Father, even the Spirit of truth, which proceedeth from the Father, He shall testify of Me..." (John 15:26 KJV). "Howbeit when He, the Spirit of truth, is come, He will guide you into all truth: for He shall not speak of himself; but whatsoever He shall hear, that shall He speak: and He will show you things to come. He shall glorify Me: for He shall receive of Mine, and shall show it unto you." (John 16:13, 14 KJV).

I hereby offer unto you some of the characteristics and qualities of Jesus Christ. This listing is by no means exhaustive. I encourage you to add other characteristics and qualities as the Holy Ghost would direct you. What does Jesus Christ mean to you?

Jesus Christ is our EPITOME OF RESPONSIBILITY! Jesus Christ is the (our) GREATEST LEADER in the history of mankind! Jesus Christ is our SOVEREIGN GOD AND PRE-EMINENT IN ALL THINGS! Jesus Christ always takes RESPONSIBILITY and ACTS in a PRO-ACTIVE fashion! Jesus Christ is ONE with the FATHER and the HOLY SPIRIT! Jesus Christ is our NEW BLOOD COVENANT! Jesus Christ is our NEW TESTAMENT! Jesus Christ is GOD INCARNATE! Jesus Christ is EMANUEL - - GOD WITH US! Jesus Christ is our PERFECT UNITY! Jesus Christ is GOD THE SON! Jesus Christ is the SON OF GOD! Jesus Christ is our CREATOR! Jesus Christ is the LIGHT of the WORLD! Jesus Christ is the LIGHT of LIFE! Jesus Christ is the BREAD of LIFE! Jesus Christ is our SUSTAINER! Jesus Christ is our HEALER! Jesus Christ is our PROVIDER! Jesus Christ CAN DO! Jesus Christ is our POSITIVE ATTITUDE! Jesus Christ is our VISION! Jesus Christ is our PURPOSE AND GOAL! Jesus Christ is our DISCIPLINE! Jesus Christ empowers us to SOAR AS THE EAGLES! Jesus Christ is our JESUS' ESTEEM! Jesus Christ is our CONFIDENCE! Jesus Christ is our HUMILITY! Jesus Christ is our OBEDIENCE! Jesus Christ is our INFLUENCE! Jesus Christ is our THANKFULNESS! Jesus Christ is our NOBILITY! Jesus Christ is our DESTINY! Jesus Christ is our STEWARD! Jesus Christ is our SERVANT! Jesus Christ is our DISCIPLINE! Jesus Christ is our SUCCESS! Jesus Christ is our SIGNIFICANCE! Jesus Christ is our LOYALTY! Jesus Christ is our ESPRIT DE CORPS! Jesus Christ is our PASSION! Jesus Christ is our PURPOSE! Jesus Christ is our INTEGRITY!

Jesus Christ is our "WALKING THE TALK"! Jesus Christ is our FAITHFULNESS! Jesus Christ is our STRENGTH! Jesus Christ is our CHARACTER! Jesus Christ is our HONOR! Jesus Christ is our PERSEVERENCE! Jesus Christ is our SACRIFICIAL LOVE! Jesus Christ is our WISDOM! Jesus Christ is our FORGIVENESS! Jesus Christ is our REDEMPTION! Jesus Christ is our COMPETENCE! Jesus Christ is our COMMITMENT TO EXCELLENCE! Jesus Christ is our EMPOWERMENT! Jesus Christ gives HIS ALL to us! Jesus Christ is our DECISIVENESS! Jesus Christ is our GREAT APOSTLE! .Jesus Christ is our EVANGELIST! Jesus Christ is our PROPHET! Jesus Christ is our KING of kings, and LORD of lords! Jesus Christ is our GREAT HIGH PRIEST! Jesus Christ is our GOOD SHEPHERD! Jesus Christ is our PREACHER! Jesus Christ is our TEACHER! Jesus Christ is our BLESSED and ONLY POTENTATE! Jesus Christ is our PERSUASION! Jesus Christ is our COMMUNICATION! Jesus Christ is our DARING and RISK! Jesus Christ is our RESULT! Jesus Christ is our ACTION! Jesus Christ is our ACTIVE, VIOLENT FAITH! Jesus Christ is our COURAGE! Jesus Christ is our ASSURANCE! Jesus Christ is our HOPE! Jesus Christ is our EXPECTANCY! Jesus Christ is our SANCTIFIER! Jesus Christ is our GLORIFIER! Jesus Christ is our PERFECT EXAMPLE! Jesus Christ is our BANNER! Jesus Christ is the CAPTAIN OF THE HOSTS OF HEAVEN — OUR COMMANDER-IN-CHIEF! Jesus Christ is our LEADER! Jesus Christ is our VICTORY! Jesus Christ is our TRIUMPH! Jesus Christ is our HERO and TERRIBLE WARRIOR! Jesus Christ is our GRACE! Jesus Christ is our MERCY SEAT! Jesus Christ is our DIVINE FAVOR! Jesus is our SAVIOR! Jesus Christ is our REDEEMER! Jesus Christ is our PEACEMAKER! Jesus Christ is our RIGHTEOUSNESS! Jesus Christ is our FREEDOM! Jesus Christ is our GOSPEL! Jesus Christ is our WORD OF GOD! Jesus Christ is our WAY! Jesus Christ is our TRUTH! Jesus Christ is our LIFE! Jesus Christ is our VICTOR! Jesus Christ is our OVERCOMER! Jesus Christ is our SHEPHERD! Jesus Christ is our BEST FRIEND and CONFIDANT! Jesus Christ is our LAMB OF GOD! Jesus Christ is our PASSOVER LAMB! Jesus Christ is our CONQUEROR! Jesus Christ is our FULLNESS and HE FILLETH

ALL IN ALL! Hallelujah! All Glory to God! "And of His fullness we have all received, and grace for grace." (John 1:16 KJV). "And I am sure that, when I come unto you, I shall come in the fullness of the blessing of the Gospel of Christ." (Romans 15:29 KJV). "And hath put all things under His feet, and gave Him to be the Head over all things to the church, Which is His body, the fullness of Him that filleth all in all." (Ephesians 1:22, 23 KJV). "And to know the love of Christ, which passeth knowledge, that ye might be filled with all the fullness of God." (Ephesians 3:19 KJV). "Till we all come in the unity of the faith, and of the knowledge of the Son of God, unto a perfect man, unto the measure of the stature of the fullness of Christ." (Ephesians 4:13 KJV). "For it pleased the Father that in Him should all fullness dwell." (Colossians 1:17 KJV). "For in Him dwelleth the all the fullness of the Godhead bodily." (Colossians 2:9 KJV).

My fellow "Conquerors for Christ", what an example and role model we have in our Lord! In Jesus we have all we need which is provided of God the Father, through the Holy Spirit! We have His authority, His power, His presence (joy) and His wisdom! We have all of the aforementioned characteristics and qualities of Jesus Christ, as His joint-heirs! If we truly have appropriated the same by the saving blood of Christ Jesus and in His Name, then we have the RESPONSIBILITY to CHOOSE to exercise our FREEDOM to be His evangelists and disciples to a lost and dying world! Let us make it our RESPONSIBILITY to be SUCCESSFUL and SIGNIFICANT in our eternal quest to be ENFORCERS OF HIS VICTORY over the devil, sin, death, sickness, oppression and possession of demons, false preachers, prophets and teachers in the apostate church, and the ways of the world! Live your personal revival today! "**The Spirit itself beareth witness with our Spirit, that we are the children of God: And if children, then heirs; heirs of God, and joint-heirs with Christ...**" (Romans 8:16, 17 KJV). "But thanks be unto God which giveth us the victory through our Lord Jesus Christ." (1 Corinthians 15:57 KJV). "Now thanks be unto God, which always causeth us to triumph in Christ, and maketh manifest the savor of His knowledge by us in every place." (2 Corinthians

2:14 KJV). "Nay, in all these things we are more than conquerors through Him that loved us." (Romans 8:37 KJV).

My fellow kings and priests of Christ Jesus, there is only one way we shall fulfill Almighty God's vision for us in the "Great Commission". We, His highly chosen Soldiers of the Cross of Christ, must exercise our free will by demonstrating our FREEDOM and RESPONSIBILITY to execute the "Great Commission", to the utmost of our abilities as the unified Army of the Light of Christ! He commands and expects as much from us. Let us be responsible to this great CAUSE OF CAUSES! Together, as the warriors of the Lion of the Tribe of Judah, we shall prevail and conquer all of the evil in the world for Jesus' sake! Let us hereby resolve to exemplify Jesus Christ in ALL things! Let us hereby resolve to be ONE IN JESUS CHRIST! "[T]hat they may be one, as We are...That they may be one; as Thou, Father, art in Me, and I in Thee, that they also may be one in Us: that the world may believe that Thou hast sent Me. And the glory which Thou gavest Me I have given them: that they may be one, even as We are one: I in them, and Thou in Me, that they may be made perfect in one; and that the world may know that Thou hast sent Me, and hast loved them, as Thou hast loved Me." (John 17:11, 21-23 KJV). Let us hereby resolve to BE and LIVE Jesus in the marketplace and beyond, in out daily lives! Let it be written! Let it be done! Oh God, we pray, in Jesus mighty Name! "And hath made us kings and priests unto God and His Father; to Him be glory and dominion for ever and ever. Amen." (Revelation 1:6 KJV). "And hath made us unto our God kings and priests: and we shall reign on the earth." (Revelation 5:10 KJV). "For by Thee I have run through a troop; and by my God have I leaped over a wall. (Proverbs 18:29 KJV).

> "But they that wait upon the Lord shall renew their strength; they shall mount up with wings as eagles; they shall run, and not be weary; and they shall walk, and not faint." (Isaiah 40:31 KJV).

Kingdom Authority & Power

～

"This know also, that in the last days perilous times will come. For men shall be lovers of their own selves, covetous, boasters, proud, blasphemers, disobedient to parents, unthankful, unholy, without natural affection, trucebreakers, false accusers, incontinent, fierce, despisers of those that are good, Traitors, heady, highminded, lovers of pleasures more than lovers of God; Having the form of godliness, but denying the power thereof: from such turn away. For of this sort are they which creep into houses, and lead captive silly women laden with sins, led away with divers lusts, Ever learning, and never able to come to the knowledge of the truth...[T]hese also resist the truth: men of corrupt minds, reprobate concerning the faith." (2 Timothy 3:1-8 KJV).

"For it is impossible for those who were once enlightened, and have tasted of the Heavenly gift, and were made partakers of the Holy Ghost, And have tasted the good Word of God, and the powers of the world to come, If they shall fall away, to renew them again unto repentance; seeing they crucify to themselves the Son of God afresh, and put Him to an open shame." (Hebrews 6:4-6 KJV).

"He that despised Moses' law died without mercy under two or three witnesses: Of how much sorer punishment, suppose ye, shall he be thought worthy, who hath trodden under foot the Son of God, and hath counted the blood of the covenant, wherewith he was sanctified, an unholy thing, and hast done despite the Spirit of grace? For we know Him that hath said, Vengeance belongeth unto Me, I will recompense, saith the Lord. And again, The Lord shall judge His people. It is a fearful thing to fall into the hands of the living God." (Hebrews 10:29-31 KJV).

The aforementioned scriptures describe the great apostasy of the church — the great falling away from Christ Jesus — in these last days. We currently are witnessing the same as false preachers, prophets and teachers pervade the body of Christ. These are men and women of the devil. These are men and women of pride. These are men and women who have sold their soul and birthright to the devil for filthy lucre (money) and popularity. These are men and women who have rebelled against Almighty God, the Cross of Christ and the power of the Resurrection. "**...Behold, to obey is better than sacrifice, and to hearken than the fat of rams. For rebellion is as the sin of witchcraft, and stubbornness is as iniquity and idolatry. Because thou hast rejected the Word of the Lord, He hath also rejected thee from being king.**" (1 Samuel 15:22, 23 KJV).

Indeed, the greatest challenge the Faithful Remnant faces in the ministry is the opposition and slander from the backslidden and apostate church. The truth of the Gospel convicts and exposes the backslidden and apostate church, as well as its leaders. Said leaders have turned their backs on the Cross of Christ. They no longer preach and teach the truth of the Gospel. In fact, they obscure the power of the cross. They have sold their souls for money. They exalt themselves instead of Christ. They walk in the pride of man and of the world instead of walking in humility, contriteness, sacrificial love and obedience. They serve to confuse and divide the church of Jesus Christ. What is more, these apostate leaders are leading the sheep who are in their care straight to hell, along with themselves! Please understand that the purpose of the Cross of Christ IS to offend and to convict and bring sinners to repentance. This IS the message of the Gospel. We must re-establish the Cross of Christ and the power of His Resurrection as the center-point of our faith, or our faith is empty and means nothing! The adversary has used these apostates as pawns and puppets to obscure the power of the Cross of Christ, which is the only way back to the Father. They refuse to preach the truth of the cross because they say it offends people and, therefore, serves to hurt their feelings, with the unhappy result that the same may not come back to the church or support the finances of the church. Hence, they preach, prophesy and teach words from man and the world (psychology, psychiatry, self-help, new age, et al), thereby itching and tickling the ears of their followers at the expense of everlasting salvation, as opposed to preaching the Word of God, which offends us in our sin and convicts us of the same by bringing us to the end of ourselves, in favor of Christ Jesus and everlasting glory. I submit to you that the aforementioned men and women have forsaken their salvation IN Christ, as they have forsaken and turned away FROM Christ. Let us be clear regarding this principle, God will not take back one's salvation but, being creatures of free choice, one can forsake one's salvation by turning away from Christ Jesus and unto themselves in their morally corrupt, putrid and self-serving pride! These backslidden and apostates are ashamed of Christ and His Gospel. They deny the Lord Jesus by preaching false idols, namely, that each individual exalt themselves above Christ Jesus by seeking the pleasures of the world. They preach that God is a loving God and that it does not matter if we sin, or how often we sin, God will forgive us. They do not preach repentance, which is the condition precedent to forgiveness. One must purpose to turn away form one's sin and follow after and apprehend Christ! God knows our heart! The Gospel of Jesus Christ is not one of toleration, but one of absolute truth! I submit to you that Almighty God IS a God of love and He proved the same by sending His only begotten Son Jesus Christ to the cross for the salvation of man! Man must repent and go through the Cross of Christ to secure forgiveness. When men and women refuse to preach the truth of the Cross of Christ and the power of His Resurrection, such self-righteousness is a fraud perpetrated against Christ and Him crucified, of the highest and most serious order! **"...The time is fulfilled, and the Kingdom of God is at hand: repent ye, and believe the Gospel." (Mark 1:15 KJV). "For the preaching of the cross... is the power of God." (1 Corinthians**

1:18 KJV). "But we preach Christ crucified...Christ, the power of God, and the wisdom of God." (1 Corinthians 1:23, 24 KJV). "For I have determined not to know any thing among you, save Jesus Christ, and Him crucified." (2 Corinthians 2:2 KJV). "...[W]oe is unto me if I preach not the Gospel!" (1 Corinthians 9:16 KJV). "For I am not ashamed of the Gospel of Christ: for it is the power of God unto salvation to every one that believeth..." (Romans 1:16 KJV). "But God forbid that I should glory, save in the cross of our Lord Jesus Christ, by whom the world is crucified unto me, and I unto the world." (Galatians 6:14 KJV). "I am crucified with Christ: nevertheless I live; yet not I, but Christ liveth in me: and the life which I now live in the flesh I live by the faith of the Son of God, who loved me, and gave Himself for me." (Galatians 2:20 KJV). "If any man will come after Me, let him deny himself, and take up his cross daily, and follow Me. (Luke 9:23 KJV). "And he that taketh not his cross, and followeth after Me, is not worthy of Me." (Matthew 10:38 KJV). "And whosoever doth not bear his cross, and come after Me, cannot be My disciple." (Luke 14:27 KJV). "For whosoever will save his life shall lose it; but whosoever shall lose his life for My sake and the Gospel's, the same shall save it. For what shall it profit a man, if he shall gain the whole world, and lose his soul? Whosoever therefore shall be ashamed of Me and of My words in this adulterous and sinful generation; of him also shall the Son of Man be ashamed, when He cometh in the glory of His Father with the holy angels." (Mark 8:35-38 KJV). "But whosoever shall deny Me before men, him will I also deny before My Father which is in Heaven." (Matthew 10:33 KJV).

The questions become, how have we come to this point? Why is there no discipline in the church? Why is the apostasy so prevalent? What has fueled the rise of so many self-serving antichrists? I submit unto you that the one of the fundamental reasons for the great falling away from Christ Jesus is the pervasive break down of Kingdom Authority in our churches, as well as, in society. I contend that our God is a God of Covenant. Covenant embodies the notion of inseparable, unbreakable relationship — a reciprocal relationship of promise. In our redemptive Covenant relationship of promise with Father God, through the shed blood of Jesus Christ, we have a two-way relational Covenant of promise, which is designed to be inseparable and unbreakable, as is the Godhead. Father God cannot lie. He will not break His Covenant with us, but will we, as creatures of choice and of pride, break our Covenant with Him? From the Old Testament through the New Testament Almighty God has sealed His Covenant relationships of promise with sacrificial blood, the ultimate climax being the perfect sacrifice offered by the perfect High Priest, the blood of the Lamb of God. By the Cross of Christ and the power of His Resurrection, we have been made His kings and priests to assert Almighty God's power on this earth against the adversary, thus enforcing the victory of Christ Jesus. Let there be no doubt, the pervasive apostasy in the church is a question of Kingdom Authority, which means that, this is a question of our dying to our pride in favor of submission and obedience to Almighty God and His Word! **"And Moses took the blood and sprinkled it on the people, and said, Behold the blood of the covenant, which the Lord hath made with you concerning all these words." (Exodus 24:8 KJV). "For this is My blood of the New Testament, which is shed for many for the remission of sins." (Matthew 26:28 KJV). "Now therefore, if ye will obey My voice indeed, and keep My covenant, then ye shall be a peculiar treasure unto Me above all people: for all earth is Mine: And ye shall be unto Me a Kingdom of priests, and an holy nation." (Exodus 19:5, 6 KJV). "For there is one God, and one mediator between God and men, the man Christ Jesus." (1 Timothy 2:5 KJV). "To whom coming, as unto a lively stone, disallowed indeed of men, but chosen of God, and precious. Ye also, as lively stones, are built up a spiritual house, a holy priesthood, to offer up spiritual sacrifices, acceptable to God by Jesus Christ. Wherefore also it is contained in the scripture, Behold, I lay in Zion a chief cornerstone, elect, precious: and he that believeth on Him shall not be confounded. Unto you therefore who believe He is precious: but unto them which be disobedient, the stone which the builders disallowed, the same is made the Head of the corner, and a Stone of Stumbling, and a Rock of Offense, even to them which stumble at the Word, being disobedient: whereunto they were also appointed. But** ye are a chosen generation, a royal priesthood, a holy nation, a peculiar people; that ye should show forth the praises of Him who hath called you out of darkness into His marvelous light." (1 Peter 2:4-9 KJV). "And from Jesus Christ, who is the Faithful Witness, and the First Begotten of the dead, and the Prince of the kings of the earth. Unto Him that loved us, and washed us from our sins in His own blood, and hath made us kings and priests unto God and His Father; to Him be glory and dominion for ever and ever. Amen." (Revelation 1:5, 6 KJV). "And hast made us unto our God kings and priests: and we shall reign on the earth." (Revelation 5:10 KJV).

In the body of Christ, this personal, relational and redemptive Covenant commands both vertical and horizontal Kingdom Authority (let us use the vertical stanchion and the horizontal crossbar of the Cross of Christ as our symbol, because it is Christ who is the center, the essence and the mediator of our relationship with God, as well as among one another), which is to be submitted to and obeyed by each and every member of the church of Christ Jesus, because the same is enforced by the Spirit of the living God! The vertical Kingdom Authority flows from the Father, the Son and the Holy Spirit into the church through the Five-Fold Ministry. These Five-Fold Ministries are the leadership of the church, as appointed by Christ Jesus, Himself. Said ministries include the offices of Apostle, Prophet, Evangelist, Pastor and Teacher. The men who hold these various offices are held to the highest of responsibility and accountability by Christ, Himself, to strictly submit to, obey and adhere to the Word of God and the direction of the Holy Spirit! They are chosen to lead with the very character, integrity, authority and power of Christ Jesus! **"...[T]he Lord hast sought Him a man after His own heart, and hath commanded him to be captain over His people." (1 Samuel 13:14 KJV).** Understand this clearly, the church is not to lead or control the leaders who are appointed by Christ! The bona-fide leaders are to lead the church and the church is to submit and obey! Amidst all of the confusion created due to rebellion in the church, the whole notion of Kingdom Authority has broken down, at the delight of the enemy! These appointed leaders of Christ are not to abdicate their responsibility to boards of Directors, Elders or Deacons! Should any of these ministers commit rebellion against Kingdom Authority and succumb to the aforementioned apostasy, then the congregants under said rebellious minister are compelled to leave the apostate ministry and find one that is faithful to Christ Jesus! The members of the church are to submit and obey the faithful, legitimate, bona fide leadership, so that order may prevail, as opposed to confusion and disorder, which is caused by rebellion against legitimate Kingdom Authority. **"For God is not the Author of confusion, but of peace, as in all churches of the saints." (1 Corinthians 14:33 KJV). "For where envying and strife is, there is confusion and every evil work." (James 3:16 KJV).** These faithful leaders represent Jesus Christ. Who would be so arrogant in their obnoxious, self-serving pride as to commit rebellion against, disrespect and abuse such highly chosen and appointed ones? Sadly, the answer is the vast majority of the members in the church, as it exists today! **"Saying, Touch not Mine anointed, and do My prophets no harm." (1 Chronicles 16: 22 KJV). "And He gave some, apostles: and some, prophets; and some, evangelists; and some, pastors and teachers; for the perfecting of the saints, for the work of the ministry, for the edifying of the body of Christ: Till we all come in the unity of the faith, and the knowledge of the Son of God, unto a perfect man, unto the measure of the stature of the fullness of Christ." (Ephesians 4:11-13 KJV). "Obey them that have rule over you, and submit yourselves: for they watch for your souls, as they that must give account, that they may do it with joy, and not grief: for that is unprofitable for you." (Hebrews 13:17 KJV). "And we beseech you, brethren, to know them which labor among you, and are over you in the Lord, and admonish you; and to esteem them very highly in love for their work's sake. And be at peace among yourselves." (1 Thessalonians 5:12, 13 KJV). "But avoid foolish questions, and genealogies, and contentions, and strivings about the law; for they are unprofitable and vain. A man that is an heretic after the first and second admonition reject; Knowing that he that is such is subverted, and sinneth, being condemned of himself." (Titus 3:9-11 KJV).**

"For ye are yet carnal: for whereas there is among you envying, and strife, and divisions, are ye not carnal, and walk as

men...is Christ divided?" (1 Corinthians 3:3; 1:13 KJV). We have witnessed that we have vertical covenant with Father God, Jesus Christ and the Holy Spirit, as well as with the Kingdom Authority that flows from the Godhead into the church via the Five-Fold Ministry. We also have horizontal Kingdom Authority among one another, as is represented by the crossbar of the Cross of Christ Jesus. Through the personal, relational and redemptive blood Covenant of Jesus Christ, Almighty God anoints men and women as His kings and priests in order that we fulfill His eternal passion and purpose for us on this earth, which is to be conformed to the image of His Son, thereby winning as many souls to Christ, as is possible. We are united unto the Godhead by the personal, relational and redemptive blood Covenant of Christ and the resultant vertical Kingdom Authority. What is more, we are united unto one another by the same personal, relational and redemptive blood Covenant of Christ and the resultant horizontal Kingdom Authority. We must esteem others better than ourselves! In order for this dynamic to be experienced fully, we must flow together in the unity of the body, in the unity of the faith, and in the unity of the Spirit. This can be achieved when we demonstrate humility, contriteness, sacrificial love and obedience, thus coming together in said unity in the knowledge of the Son of God! This is why it is imperative that the church re-establish the blood stained banner of the Cross of Jesus Christ and the power of His Resurrection as the center point of our faith, without which, we simply cannot know the King of kings and the Lord of lords! Only in knowing Christ Jesus through the cross, can we know the perfect unity and oneness of the Godhead. Only by exalting Jesus Christ and recommitting to the authority of the Word of God, will we have the last days revival of the church of Jesus Christ! Only then will we be empowered to overcome all apostasy, divisions, factions and denominational differences, in favor of Christ's conquering, victorious and glorious church! This IS the WAY of Revival! Hallelujah! **"That He might present it to Himself a glorious church, not having spot or wrinkle, or any such thing; but that it should be holy and without blemish." (Ephesians 5:27 KJV).** Hallelujah! All Glory to God! **"And Jonathan said to David, Go in peace, forasmuch as we have sworn both of us in the Name of the Lord,**

saying, The Lord be between me and thee, and between my seed and thy seed forever..." (1 Samuel 20:42 KJV). "Now I beseech you, brethren, by the Name of our Lord Jesus Christ, that ye all speak the same thing, and that there be no divisions among you; but that ye be perfectly joined together in the same mind and in the same judgment." (1 Corinthians 1:10 KJV). "That there should be no schism in the body; but that the members should have the same care one for another." (1 Corinthians 12:25 KJV). "For as the body is one, and hath many members, and all the members of that one body, being many, are one body: so also is Christ. For by one Spirit are we all baptized into one body... and have been all made to drink into one Spirit." (1 Corinthians 12:13, 14 KJV). "For as we have many members in one body, and all members have not the same office: so we, being many, are one body in Christ, and every one members one of another." (Romans 12:4, 5 KJV). "But he that is joined unto the Lord is one spirit." (1 Corinthians 6:17 KJV). "In whom ye also are builded together for a habitation of God through the Spirit." (Ephesians 2:22 KJV). "Endeavoring to keep the unity of the Spirit in the bond of peace. There is one body, and one Spirit, even as ye are called in one hope of your calling; One Lord, one faith, one baptism, One God and Father of all, who is above all, and through all, and in you all." (Ephesians 4:3-6 KJV). "And grieve not the Holy Spirit of God, whereby ye are sealed unto the day of redemption. Let all bitterness, and wrath, and anger, and clamor, and evil speaking, be put away from you, with all malice: And be ye kind to one another, tenderhearted, forgiving one another, even as God for Christ's sake hath forgiven you." (Ephesians 4:30-32 KJV). "Likewise, ye younger, submit yourselves unto the elder. Yea, all of you be subject one to another, and be clothed with humility: for God resisteth the proud, and giveth grace unto the humble. Humble yourselves therefore under the mighty hand of God, that He may exalt you in due time: Casting all your care upon Him, for He careth for you." (1 Peter 5:5-7 KJV). "Fulfill ye my joy, that ye be likeminded, having the same love, being of one accord, of one mind. Let nothing be done through strife or vainglory; but in lowliness of mind let each esteem other better than themselves. Let this mind be in you, which was also in Christ Jesus..." (Philippians 2:2, 3, 5 KJV). "And Jesus knew their thoughts, and said unto them, Every kingdom divided against itself is brought to desolation; and every city or house divided against itself shall not stand." (Matthew 12:25 KJV). "...[T]hat they may be one, as We are. That they all may be one; as Thou, Father art in Me, and I in Thee, that they also may be one in Us: that the world may believe that Thou hast sent Me. And the glory which Thou gavest Me I have given them; that they may be one, even as We are one: I in them, and Thou in Me, that they may be made perfect in one; and the world may know that Thou hast sent Me, and hast loved them, as Thou hast loved Me." (John 17:11, 21-23 KJV).

"But they that wait upon the Lord shall renew their strength; they shall mount up with wings as eagles; they shall run, and not be weary; and they shall walk, and not faint." (Isaiah 40:31 KJV).

Evangelizing, Discipleship and Witnessing

Evangelizing, discipleship and witnessing are all about building personal relationships in Christ Jesus. Indeed, the whole notion of Christ's Church, His Kingdom, the Body of Christ, the Army of the Light is about establishing and nurturing a vibrant personal relationship with our Lord and Savior Jesus Christ, and sharing His Gospel with our fellow men, women and children, thus advancing His "Great Commission". Christ founded His Church upon the Apostles and they were commanded to build relationships with people, preach the Gospel and witness to them regarding Jesus Christ. Christ's Church is all about relationships — divinely connected — one Body in Christ — purchased in His precious blood. We, as the highly chosen "Conquerors for Christ", are responsible for the faithful execution of the same! **"According to the grace of God which is given unto me, as a wise masterbuilder, I have laid the foundation, and another buildeth thereon. But let every man take heed how he buildeth thereupon." (1 Corinthians 3:10 KJV). "For as the body is one, and hath many members, and all the members of that one body, being many, are one body: so also is Christ. For by one Spirit we are all baptized into one body...and have been all made to drink of the same Spirit." (1 Corinthians 12:12, 13 KJV). "But ye shall receive power, after that the Holy Ghost is come upon you: and ye shall be witnesses unto Me both in Jerusalem, and in all Judea, and in Samaria, and unto the uttermost part of the earth. (Acts 1:8 KJV).**

Almighty God is providing us with so many glorious opportunities to build relationships for Jesus. He provides us with one-on-one evangelizing, discipleship and witnessing opportunities. He provides us with group evangelizing, discipleship and witnessing opportunities. Pray that Abba Daddy shall make you a divine appointment wherever you are! As bona fide Christian men women and children duly purchased in the precious blood of the Lamb of God, and indwelled and infilled by the Holy Ghost, we are of the same mind as Jesus, thus relationship building comes very natural to us because we are doing the work of our Lord. We are being Jesus to them because Jesus is a supernatural extension of you and me, by the power of the Holy Spirit! We are offering them a personal relationship with our Lord and Savior! Since our purpose and goal in life is to be changed into the character and image of Christ Jesus, the more we demonstrate all nine elements of the fruit of the Spirit, the more people will be drawn to us for witness unto Christ! Remember, the more we live the fruit of the Spirit, the more the power of the Holy Spirit flows through us as rivers of living waters in blessing, victory and Resurrection life! This IS the WAY Jesus Christ becomes a supernatural extension of who we are! Hallelujah! **"...But we have the mind of Christ." (1 Corinthians 2:16 KJV). "But ye shall receive power, after that the Holy Ghost is come upon you: and ye shall be witnesses unto Me both in Jerusalem, and in all Judea, and in Samaria, and unto the uttermost part of the earth." (Acts 1:8 KJV). "For whom He did foreknow, He also did predestinate to be conformed to the image of His Son..." (Romans 8:29 KJV). "But the fruit of the Spirit is love, joy peace, long-suffering, gentleness, goodness, faith, Meekness, temperance: against such there is no law." (Galatians 5:22, 23 KJV).**

Allow me to share some specific techniques to assist you in facilitating your relationship building, hence your relationship evangelizing, discipleship and witnessing for Jesus.

The condition precedent to success and significance in this regard is to place Jesus' esteem in each prospect — in other words — to become a friend and confidant to the prospect by showing honor, respect and reverence. This is done by demonstrating empathy, seeking first to understand the conditions and circumstances of the individual, then to be understood by addressing the same with the Gospel of Jesus Christ! Remember that empathy is the sharing of the thoughts, feelings and emotions of another in order to understand their situation. Empathy must be contrasted and distinguished from the notion of sympathy, which is actually identifying and agreeing with another's situation. Sympathy endorses the situation, whereas empathy seeks to understand the situation, without approving, endorsing or sanctioning the same. This is a crucial distinction and must be recognized to enable us to build effective relationships in order to lead people to Christ Jesus. By understanding another's situation, one is able to identify the needs of the individual and, because you have not sympathized, thus condoning the same, you are able to offer the solution to their situation, namely Christ Jesus! This is done by appropriately applying each of Christ's benefits to the person's needs (the primary need and, hence, benefit being salvation), with the divine purpose and love of our Savior. As **John 17:22, 26 declares: "And the glory which thou gavest Me I have given them; that they may be one, even as We are one...And I have declared unto them Thy Name and will declare it: that the love wherewith Thou hast loved Me may be in them, and I in them." "...I am the way, the truth, and the life: no man cometh unto the Father, but by Me." (John 14:6 KJV).**

The key to empathy is to diligently listen to what people have to say, by the power of the Holy Spirit. We all know that people love to talk about themselves. After all, whom do they better know? This phenomenon also goes to the proposition that, as human beings, we need fellowship, we need nurturing, we need community — we need the Body of Christ! There are two dialog-initiating processes, which are very effective, natural and efficient — namely — SPIN & POGO, as developed and taught by Mr. Zig Ziegler. Bear in mind that SPIN & POGO can be utilized over the phone, one-on-one, or in-group ministry. Open-ended questions (feeling and thinking questions) should be employed to identify the wants, needs, desires, ideas and opinions of prospects. Thus, utilize questions beginning with "Who", "What", "When", "Where", "How", and "Why" to allow the prospects the requisite freedom to take the answers where they desire. Utilize closed ended questions to keep your prospects in a certain area for clarification and embellishment. For this purpose, employ questions such as, "Would you tell me more about...?", or

"That's fascinating. What do you mean by...?" Be very conversational — not confrontational — with a pleasant, calming, and reassuring voice tonality. Smile! See Jesus in them -- then demonstrate Jesus to them!

To SPIN someone, you merely ask the following questions to establish meaningful conversation and dialog:

S — What is your SITUATION professionally/personally?
P — What PROBLEMS/challenges/issues does this SITUATION present/create?
I — What are the IMPLICATIONS of those PROBLEMS/challenges/issues?
N — What do you perceive as your NEEDS to remedy these PROBLEMS/IMPLICATIONS?

Once they have identified their NEEDS, we address each NEED with the BENEFITS of Jesus Christ and His Gospel!

We also use the POGO technique interchangeably with the SPIN:

P — ASK them about themselves PERSONALLY.
O — ASK them about their ORGANIZATION or PROFESSIONAL life.
G — ASK them to identify their GOALS, both PERSONALLY and ORGANIZATIONALLY.
O — ASK them to identify their OBSTACLES.

Once they have identified their OBSTACLES, we address each OBSTACLE with the BENEFITS of Jesus Christ and His Gospel! All Glory to God!

Allow me to share salvation scriptures that we share whenever and wherever we evangelize, disciple and witness. Said scriptures lead the WAY unto everlasting salvation through the Cross of Christ and the power of His Resurrection!

"Jesus answered and said unto him, Verily, verily, I say unto thee, Except a man be born again, he cannot see the Kingdom of God." (John 3:3 KJV).

"For all have sinned, and come short of the glory of God..." (Romans 3:23 KJV).

"For the wages of sin is death; but the gift of God is eternal life through Jesus Christ our Lord. (Romans 6:23 KJV).

"...Sirs, what must I do to be saved...Believe on the Lord Jesus Christ, and thou shalt be saved, and thy house." (Acts 16:30, 31 KJV).

"Jesus saith unto him, I am the way, the truth, and the life: no man commeth unto the Father, but by Me." (John 14:6 KJV).

"For God so loved the world, that He gave His only begotten Son, that whosoever believeth in Him should not perish, but have everlasting life." (John 3:16 KJV).

"That if thou shalt confess with thy mouth the Lord Jesus, and shalt believe in thine heart that God raised Him from the dead, thou shalt be saved. For with the heart man believeth unto righteousness; and with the mouth confession is made unto salvation...For whosoever shall call upon the Name of the Lord shall be saved." (Romans 10:9, 10, 13 KJV).

These techniques work! I have employed them for years and they always prove extremely effective. They afford us the opportunity to become another's friend and confidant, which is the condition precedent to establishing a long term WIN-WIN relationship — even for eternity. This is the essence of Christian evangelism, discipleship and witnessing! **"Praising God, and having favor with all the**

people. And the Lord added to the church daily such as should be saved." (Acts 2:47 KJV).

After you have shared the aforementioned scriptures, lead them in the prayer of salvation pursuant to said scriptures: "Father God, I know that I am a sinner. I repent from my sins. Please forgive me of my sins. Jesus Christ, You died for me on the cross. Jesus, I believe that God raised You from the dead. I confess You, Jesus, as Lord of my life. Jesus, please come into my heart and save me. Thank You, Jesus, I am born again in Your precious blood, by the power of the Holy Spirit, and I belong to You for evermore! And Jesus, I ask You to make me a mighty "Conqueror for Christ" in Your Army of the Light! Amen!"

We encourage you to use these techniques and scriptures. They are anointed! They work! Millions of men, women and children have come through the Cross of Christ and received Him as Lord and Savior of their lives via our ministries, utilizing the same! Hallelujah!

Christ Jesus, as Head of the church, has chosen us as His kings and priests. He has chosen us to make provision for His vision to support His Church with the income we generate by conquering the marketplace and beyond, in our daily lives. With said provision, we then support and underwrite the preaching of the Gospel of Jesus Christ unto all nations! Let us, the "Conquerors for Christ", highly resolve not only to support and underwrite the same, but to BE the preachers and teachers of the Gospel of Jesus Christ unto the world! Hallelujah! **"And hath put all things under His feet, and gave Him to be the Head over all things to the church, Which is His body, the fullness of Him that filleth all in all." (Ephesians 1:22,23 KJV). "And hath made us unto our God kings and priests: and we shall reign on the earth." (Revelation 5:10 KJV). "And Jesus spake onto them, saying, All power is given unto Me in Heaven and in earth. Go ye therefore, and teach all nations, baptizing them in the Name of the Father, and of the Son, and of the Holy Ghost: Teaching them to observe all things whatsoever I have commanded you: and, lo, I am with you always, even unto the end of the world. Amen. (Matthew 28:18-20 KJV).**

As Almighty God's saints on earth, we have been "commissioned" to establish Jesus' line of conquest and victory from the grassroots of our neighborhoods to every nation and the inhabitants thereof. The key to being successful and significant in our divine crusade is to build long-term win-win relationships with our fellow men, women and children, in Jesus' mighty Name! O, let our quest be to evangelize, disciple and witness unto Jesus Christ and His Gospel to the lost and dying world, with the sword of the Spirit! Let us faithfully execute our "Great Commission", with the expectancy that all peoples of the earth shall recognize, acknowledge and confess that Jesus Christ is Lord to the glory of God the Father! Hallelujah! To this end, **Philippians 2:2,5,7,8,9,10,11 is so vividly instructive: "Fulfill ye My joy, that ye be likeminded, having the same love, being of one accord, of one mind. Let this mind be in you, which was also in Christ Jesus. But made Himself of no reputation and took upon Him the form of a servant, and was made in the likeness of men: And being found in fashion as a man, He humbled Himself, and became obedient unto death, even the death of the cross. Wherefore God also hath highly exalted Him, and given Him a Name which is above every name. That at the Name of Jesus every knee should bow, of things in heaven, and things in earth, and things under the earth; And that every tongue should confess that Jesus Christ is Lord, to the glory of God the Father."** Let it be written. Let it be done. Amen!

> **"But they that wait upon the Lord shall renew their strength; they shall mount up with wings as eagles; they shall run, and not be weary; and they shall walk, and not faint." (Isaiah 40:31 KJV).**

Faithful Obedience

~~~

"**Behold, to obey is better than sacrifice...for rebellion is as the sin of witchcraft, and stubbornness is as iniquity and idolatry." (1 Samuel 15:22, 23 KJV).** Praise Jesus Christ that He was submissive and obedient to the Father, even unto the death of the cross. Pray tell, what would be the condition of sinful man had Christ disobeyed and rebelled against the Father? But for the death of Christ Jesus, there would have been no Resurrection, no way unto resurrection life, no way unto redemption, no way unto salvation, no way unto reconciliation, no way unto repentance, no way unto forgiveness and therefore, no way unto eternal life with Father God in Glory! Our destiny would have been only death, damnation and eternal separation from the Father. Our Lord and Savior's example is one of humility, contriteness, sacrificial love and obedience. He esteemed others higher than Himself in order to carry out the divine and perfect will of the Father for the salvation and redemption of those who would come in humility, contriteness and repentance unto the Cross of Christ, seeking forgiveness, and receiving eternal salvation by His shed blood. Because of the "Faithful Obedience" of Christ Jesus, we are justified and made righteous! Thank You, Jesus, for your "Faithful Obedience"! Hallelujah! **"Jesus sayeth unto him, I am the way, the truth, and the life: no man cometh unto the Father, but by Me." (John 14:6 KJV). "I am the resurrection, and the life...And whosoever liveth and believeth in Me shall never die. Believeth thou this?" (John 11:25, 26 KJV). Greater love hath no man than this, that a man lay down his life for his friends." (John 15:13 KJV). "Saying, Father, if Thou be willing, remove this cup from Me: nevertheless not My will, but

Thine be done." (Luke 22:42 KJV). "For by one man's disobedience many were made sinners, so by the obedience of one shall many be made righteous." (Romans 5:19 KJV). "And being found in fashion as a man, he humbled Himself, and became obedient unto death, even the death of the cross. Wherefore God also hath highly exalted him, and given Him a Name which is above every name: That at the Name of Jesus every knee should bow...And that every tongue should confess that Jesus Christ is Lord, to the glory of God the Father." (Philippians 2:8-11 KJV). "Looking unto Jesus the Author and Finisher of our faith; Who for the joy that was set before Him, endured the cross, despising the shame, and is set down at the right hand of the throne of God." (Hebrews 12:2 KJV).

Almighty God always honors our "Faithful Obedience" to his Word. As Christian men and women, we have been chosen to serve in the Army of the Light of Jesus Christ in the marketplace and beyond, in our daily lives. Almighty God has "Commissioned" us as officers in His Son's Army. Jesus has entrusted us with His power and authority to assert the same against the enemy, thus enforcing the Victory of Christ Jesus on the Cross and the power of His Resurrection! "According to the glorious Gospel of the blessed God, which was committed to my trust." (1 Timothy 1:11 KJV). "For the preaching of the cross...is the power of God." (1 Corinthians 1:18 KJV). "Behold, I give you power to tread on serpents and scorpions, and over all the power of the enemy: and nothing shall by any means hurt you." (Luke 10:19 KJV). "But thanks be unto God which giveth us the victory through our Lord Jesus Christ." (1 Corinthians 15:57 KJV). The condition precedent for our success and significance is our "Faithful Obedience" in the performance and execution of the duties commensurate with said "Commission". Such duties include activating and demonstrating our violent faith while making full use of the work of evangelism and discipleship with which Christ Jesus has commanded us. All such work glorifies God and honors Jesus. The work of Christ is our mandate. We glorify Almighty God by engaging the creative genius of our Creator, who abides in us, by the power of the Holy Spirit, to that end. God has given us, His kings and priests, the command to make provision for His vision and preach the Gospel of Jesus Christ to everyone. This is our call to duty! This is our call to glorify the Father! This is our call to honor Jesus Christ! This is our call to "Faithful Obedience"! Hallelujah! **"...[T]he Kingdom of Heaven suffereth violence, and the violent take it by force." (Matthew 11:12 KJV). "... [B]ut a doer of the work, this man shall be blessed in his deed." (James 1:25 KJV). "Even so faith, if it hath not works is dead, being alone...I will show thee my faith by my works." (James 2:17,18 KJV). "And hath made us unto our God kings and priests: and we shall reign on the earth." (Revelation 5:10 KJV). "But watch thou in all things, endure afflictions, do the work of an evangelist, make full proof of thy ministry." (2 Timothy 4:5 KJV). "And He said unto them, Go ye into all the world, and preach the Gospel to every creature." (Mark 16:15 KJV).**

When we perform our duties as Christ's "Commissioned" officers, He honors us as we honor Him. He promises to do so in Holy Scripture. As believers it is incumbent upon us to have consummate faith in His promises. When we obey and serve Christ through our work of evangelism and discipleship, our Father promises to honor us with prosperity and pleasures, spiritual and otherwise. **"If they obey and serve Him, they shall spend their days in prosperity, and their years in pleasures." (Job 35:11 KJV).** God's will is not always easily obtained, but His will is PERFECT, and His will is always done! Being one with Him requires our "Faithful Obedience" to His Word at all times. Thank God for the Holy Spirit! With the Holy Spirit indwelling and infilling us, and enduing us with His power, conviction, counsel and the perfect will of God, all things are possible in the name of Jesus Christ! **"But ye shall receive power, after that the Holy Ghost is come upon you: and ye shall be witnesses unto Me both in Jerusalem, and in all Judea, and in Samaria, and unto the uttermost part of the earth." (Acts 1:8 KJV). "I can do all things through Christ which strengtheneth me." (Philippians 4:13 KJV).** Let us take up the Sword of the Spirit and conquer the enemy standing shoulder to shoulder with Jesus Christ, our Commander-in-Chief! **"And take...the sword of the Spirit, which is the Word of God." (Ephesians 6:17: KJV).**

Let us highly resolve to faithfully execute our "Great Commission" in the marketplace and beyond, in our daily lives, with all passion and dispatch! Let us hereby resolve to exalt, honor and glorify God's choosing us as His "Commissioned" officers to serve in the "Great Commission" of Jesus Christ, by our "Faithful Obedience", thereby executing our battle plan in our noble "Commission" to the fullest! Let us overcome the enemy and enforce the VICTORY of Jesus Christ at every turn! Let it be written. Let it be done. **"Nay, in all these things we are more than conquerors through Him that loved us." (Romans 8:37 KJV).** "Peace be unto you: as My Father has sent Me, even so send I you." (John 20:21 KJV). "Wherefore I put thee in remembrance that thou stir up the gift of God, which is in thee..." (2 Timothy 1:6 KJV). " If a man love Me, he will keep My words: and My Father will love him, and We will come unto him, and make Our abode with him." (John 14:23 KJV). " If ye love Me, keep My commandments." (John 14:15 KJV).

> **"But they that wait upon the Lord shall renew their strength; they shall mount up with wings as eagles; they shall run, and not be weary; and they shall walk, and not faint." (Isaiah 40:31 KJV).**

HIS Service — The Road Best Traveled

As Almighty God's kings and priests of the marketplace and beyond, in our daily lives, we are blessed abundantly to be chosen in His service here on earth, as it is in heaven. Jesus Christ has commanded us to take up His Cross, as He leads us on the road to Calvary and beyond, in our daily service unto Him, by demonstrating, living and enforcing His victory in the everlasting freedom of His precious, saving blood — the blood of the Lamb of God! Jesus Christ has given you and me the keys to the Kingdom of Heaven — the Gospel of Jesus Christ! With the Gospel comes all of the power and authority of the Jesus Christ to be more than conquerors in all warfare against the enemy! **"And I will give unto thee the keys of the Kingdom of Heaven: and whatsoever thou shalt bind on earth shall be bound in Heaven: and whatsoever thou shalt loose on earth shall be loosed in Heaven." (Matthew 16:19 KJV). "If any man will come after Me, let him deny himself, and take up his cross daily, and follow Me." (Luke 9:23 KJV). "And he that taketh not his cross, and followeth after Me, is not worthy of Me." (Matthew 10:38 KJV). "And whosoever doth not bear his cross, and come after Me, cannot be My disciple." (Luke 14:27 KJV). "And hath made us unto our God kings and priests: and we shall reign on the earth." (Revelation 5:10 KJV). "...Behold the Lamb of God Who taketh away the sin of the world." (John 1:29 KJV). "...[T]he Lamb slain from the foundation of the world." (Revelation 13:8 KJV). "Nay, in all these things we are more than conquerors through Him that loved us." (Romans 8:37 KJV).**

By following the perfect example of Christ Jesus and being faithful and loyal to Him, we pursue, journey and live, "His Service — The Road Best Traveled", thus achieving success and significance in the eyes of Almighty God. We have been called unto salvation by the preaching of the Cross of Christ. The question becomes, whether we will pay the price to be chosen by Christ Jesus as His Faithful Remnant and friends — His inner circle and "Conquerors for Christ", if you will — by returning to the Cross of Christ every day and dying to self, pride, sin, sin nature, the adversary, and the ways of the world, thus being changed into the character and image of Jesus Christ, from glory to glory. This is the "Way" we live a lifestyle of repentance — a lifestyle of personal revival — and we bear lasting and ripe fruit unto the Lord! All Glory to God! **"For many are called, but few are chosen." (Matthew 22:14 KJV). "...[T]hat ye present your bodies a living sacrifice, holy, acceptable unto God, which is your reasonable service." (Romans 12:1 KJV). "These shall make war with the Lamb, and the Lamb shall overcome them: for He is Lord of lords, and King of kings: and they that are with Him are called, and chosen, and faithful." (Revelation 17:14 KJV). "For the preaching of the cross...is the power of God." (1 Corinthians 1:18 KJV). "But we preach Christ crucified...Christ the power of God and the wisdom of God." (1 Corinthians 23, 24 KJV). "I am crucified with Christ: nevertheless I live; yet not I, but Christ liveth in me: and the life which I now live in the flesh I live by the faith of the Son of God, who loved me, and gave Himself for me." (Galatians 2:20 KJV). "Greater love hath no man than this, that a man lay down his life for his friends. Ye are My friends, if ye do whatever I command you. Henceforth I call you not servants, for the servant knoweth not what his lord doeth: but I have called you friends; for all things I have heard of My Father I have made known unto you. Ye have not chosen Me, but I have chosen you, and ordained you, that ye should go and bring forth fruit, and that your fruit shall remain..." (John 15:13-16 KJV). "Ye shall know them by their fruits...Wherefore by their fruits ye shall know them." (Matthew 7:16, 19 KJV).**

His service, the "Great Commission", commands us to evangelize and witness to as many people as possible, in order to bring them to the end of themselves at the Cross of Christ, in favor of the saving blood of Christ Jesus. When we exercise our freedom in Christ Jesus and proclaim Him to the lost and dying men, women and children of this world, we love them, as does Jesus. It is the great agape, unconditional, undeserved and sacrificial love with which Christ loves all of mankind — the love that sent Him to the cross! **"If the Son therefore shall make you free, ye shall be free indeed." (John 8:36 KJV). "Hereby perceive we the love of God, because He laid down His life for us: and we ought to lay down our lives for the brethren." (1 John 3:16 KJV). "Herein is love, not that we loved God, but He loved us, and sent His Son to be the propitiation for our sins." (1 John 4:10 KJV).** By placing Jesus' esteem in the lost and dying people of the world, as well as our brethren, we honor their potential brilliance and worth in Christ and, at the same time, reinforce the same in ourselves. Indeed — we reap what we sow. **"If there be therefore any consolation in Christ, if any fellowship of the Spirit, if any bowels and mercies, Fulfill ye my joy, that ye be likeminded, having the same love, being of one accord, of one mind. Let nothing be done through strife or vainglory; but in lowliness of mind let each esteem other better than themselves. Look not every man on his own things, but every man also on the things of others. Let this mind be in you, which was also in Christ Jesus..." (Philippians 2:1-5 KJV). "Be not deceived; God is not mocked: for whatsoever a man soweth, that shall he also reap." (Galatians 6:7 KJV).**

Fellow "Conquerors for Christ", Almighty God has blessed us with one of His most compelling platforms with which to fulfill the "Great Commission" of Jesus Christ our Lord and Savior. That blessing is the marketplace and beyond, in our daily lives. We must exploit the same in the character of Christ! Jesus Christ has given us the perfect example — The Way — to spread the Gospel from the grassroots of our neighborhoods to the whole of the world — to every nation — to every fellow human being! You see, "His Service — The Road Best Traveled", with Christ Jesus as our Commander-in-Chief, involves the ever changing, ongoing process of sanctification, which is our being changed into the same image as Jesus Christ, from glory to glory, even as by the Spirit of the Lord. This is leadership by example! The quality, success and significance of our journey together in Him, depends on our demonstrating the positive attitude, unified faith and a win-win mentality of Christ, Himself, while executing our shared vision which has been inspired by the Holy Spirit. We are chosen to declare the Name above all names — Jesus Christ — to a lost and dying world! We must remain faithful and true to our "Great Commission" by demonstrating, living and proclaiming Christ, thus being His leaders by example. We must remember to admonish the multitudes that the road — "The Way" — to Heaven is narrow, as is its very entry way — "The Gate" to the Kingdom of Heaven, and few find the same, because they do not pursue a lifestyle of repentance and sanctification. Only those who pursue Christ and determine to grow up into Him — pursue holiness and sanctification — shall enter through "The Gate" of the Kingdom of Heaven. We must warn the multitudes of the false preachers, prophets and teachers in the apostate church, who lead unwary sheep to slaughter by propounding lies from hell, and tickle ears for filthy lucre, to exalt themselves and their sinful pride. These do not preach a lifestyle of repentance, indeed, they preach a license to sin, as they convolute the doctrine of grace and freedom in Christ! Such are workers of iniquity and shall be cast away by Christ Jesus! **"Be kindly affectioned one to another with brotherly love; in honor preferring one another; not slothful in business; fervent in spirit; serving the Lord." (Romans 12:10,11 KJV). "But as He which hath called you is holy, so be ye holy in all manner of conversation; Because it is written, Be ye holy; for I am holy." (1 Peter 1:15, 16 KJV). "Follow...holiness, without which no man shall see the Lord." (Hebrews 12:14 KJV). "For there are many unruly and vain talkers and deceivers...Whose mouths must be stopped, who subvert whole houses, teaching things which the ought not, for filthy lucre's sake...Wherefore rebuke them sharply...They profess that they know God; but in works they deny Him, being abominable, and disobedient, and unto every good work reprobate." (Titus 1:10, 11, 13, 16 KJV). "Enter ye in at the strait gate: for wide is the gate, and broad is the way, that leadeth to destruction, and many there be which go in thereat: Because strait is the gate, and narrow is the way, which leadeth** unto life, and few there be that find it. Beware of false prophets, which come to you in sheep's clothing, but inwardly they are ravening wolves. Ye shall know them by their fruits...Wherefore by their fruits ye shall know them. Not every one that saith unto Me, Lord, Lord, shall enter into the Kingdom of Heaven; but he that doeth the will of My Father which is in Heaven. Many will say to Me in that day, Lord, Lord, have we not prophesied in Thy Name? and in Thy Name have cast out devils? and in Thy Name done many wonderful works? And then will profess unto them, I never knew you: depart from Me, ye that work iniquity." (Matthew 7:13-16; 20-23 KJV).

In our holy service to Almighty God in the marketplace and beyond, in our daily lives, let us ever strive for the excellence of Jesus Christ as we lead in the pursuit of Christlikeness, while living and sharing the truths and character of our Lord and Savior. Let us be bold for Jesus and enforce His Victory by choosing to honor and serve Him as His disciples and evangelists, thereby advancing our "Great Commission" given from the Throne of God! In this way we choose to honor "HIS Service — The Road Best Traveled". Jesus Christ lives! Jesus Christ is Lord! Jesus Christ is Savior! Hallelujah! "...[B]ut as for me and my house, we will serve the Lord." (Joshua 24:15 KJV). "I press toward the mark of the prize of the high calling of God in Christ Jesus." (Philippians 3:14 KJV). Let us purpose to dutifully and faithfully execute our "Great Commission" as the "Conquerors for Christ" in His Army of the Light! The mighty Name of Jesus Christ is our sovereign battle cry! "Give us souls lest we die, that the Lamb who was slain might receive the reward of His suffering, as the glory perfects the unity, and the unity proclaims the glory!" Amen and Hallelujah! "Ye are the light of the world." (Matthew 5:14 KJV). "...Go ye into all the world and preach the Gospel to every creature." (Mark 16:15 KJV). "Wherefore God also hath highly exalted Him, and given Him a Name which is above every name: That at the Name of Jesus every knee should bow, of things in Heaven, and things in earth, and things under the earth; And that every tongue should confess that Jesus Christ is Lord, to the glory of God the Father." (Philippians 2;9-11 KJV).

Let us soar as the eagles in Father God's Heavenlies, by the power of the Holy Spirit! All Glory to God!

"But they that wait upon the Lord shall renew their strength; they shall mount up with wings as eagles; they shall run, and not be weary; and they shall walk, and not faint." (Isaiah 40:31 KJV).

Why Ambassadors for Jesus Christ Are Relevant

I respectfully submit to you that our Lord and Savior Jesus Christ is relevant and appropriate, for all time. Jesus Christ and His Gospel are practical and have a great bearing on every matter at hand, as relating to our present condition and our eternal salvation. Being relevant, then, Jesus Christ and His Gospel are highly significant and highly important to all situations and circumstances. He is omniscient, omnipotent, omnipresent and pre-eminent in all things! He continues to exert supernaturally, by the power of His Cross and Resurrection, positive influence in connection with and, therefore, has profound effect on, the condition of the day and time in which we live, as well as for all eternity! When we submit and obey Christ Jesus and His Word, thus yielding to His Holy Spirit as His faithful ambassadors, we are, as His joint-heirs, empowered to the same social relevance, as is Christ Jesus! Hallelujah! **"And Jesus came and spake unto them, saying, All power is given unto Me in Heaven and in earth. Go ye therefore, and teach all nations, baptizing them in the Name of the Father, and of the Son, and of the Holy Ghost: Teaching them to observe all things whatsoever I have commanded you: and, lo, I am with you always, even unto the end of the world." (Matthew 28:18-20 KJV). "And He is the Head of the body, the church: who is the beginning, the first-born from the dead; that in all things He might have the pre-eminence. And it pleased the Father that in Him should all fullness dwell. And, having made peace through the blood of the cross, by Him to reconcile all things unto Himself; by Him, I say, whether they be things in earth, or things in Heaven."**

(Colossians 1:18-20 KJV). "The Spirit itself beareth witness with our spirit, that we are the children of God: And if children, then heirs; heirs of God, and joint-heirs with Christ..." (Romans 8:16, 17 KJV). "Now then we are ambassadors for Christ, as though God did beseech you by us: we pray you in Christ's stead, be ye reconciled to God. For He hath made Him to be sin for us, who knew no sin; that we might be made the righteousness of God in Him." (2 Corinthians 5:20, 21 KJV).

Do you know of any man who was, and is, more relevant than Jesus Christ? "I am Alpha and Omega, the beginning and the ending, saith the Lord, which is, and which was, and which is to come, the Almighty." (Revelation 1:8 KJV). "Jesus Christ the same yesterday, and today, and forever." (Hebrews 13:8 KJV). Jesus becomes relevant in every situation we encounter. When He was on this earth, often He spoke in parables and His disciples learned great practical lessons. Parables convey spiritual truth through a series of earthly comparisons. Jesus would share the parable and then explain its meaning unto his disciples. In this way, He was able to withhold further truth of Himself and the Kingdom of Heaven from those in the crowds who had proved deaf to His Gospel. Through His teachings, which are relevant to all hearers' present and eternal condition, Christ, through His disciples, is able to foster His Gospel to the lost and dying world. Thus, Jesus is able to influence and affect His world in a positive fashion and advance His Gospel by being socially appropriate, practical and relevant in the matters of the day, as the same relate to eternal salvation. Jesus Christ is relevant for all time! Glory to God! **"And the disciples came, and said unto Him, Why speakest Thou unto them in parables? He answered and said unto them, Because it is given unto you to know the mysteries of the Kingdom of Heaven, but to them it is not given."** (Matthew 13:10, 11 KJV). "For I am not ashamed of the Gospel of Christ: for it is the power of God unto salvation to every one that believeth; to the Jew first, and also to the Greek." (Romans 1:16 KJV). "Jesus saith unto him, I am the way, the truth, and the life: no man cometh unto the Father, but by Me." (John 14:6 KJV). "But we preach Christ crucified...Christ the power of God, and the wisdom of God." (1 Corinthians 1:23, 24 KJV).

Now let us examine the following scripture and apply its relevance to the marketplace and beyond, in our daily lives: **"For though I be free from all men, yet have I made myself servant unto all, that I might gain the more. And unto the Jews I became as a Jew, that I might gain the Jews; to them that are under the law, as under the law, that I might gain them that are under the law; To them that are without law, as without law, (being not without law to God, but under the law of Christ,) that I might gain them that are without law. To the weak I became weak, that I might gain the weak; I am made all things to all men, that I might by all means save some. And this I do for the Gospel's sake, that I might be partaker thereof with you". (1 Corinthians 9:19-23 KJV).** Paul is arguing the notion of relevancy. Without losing or compromising his belief in Christ or the Gospel, Paul became appropriate unto those whom he was evangelizing and discipleship. Paul was all about social relevancy so that he could significantly influence his world via the preaching of the Gospel of Jesus Christ. Paul identified with his listeners and their condition (empathy) and understood the same, so as to be practical in his preaching and thereby, apply the Gospel to their present and eternal condition. **"For though I preach the Gospel, I have nothing to glory of: for necessity is laid upon me; yea, woe is unto me, if I preach not the Gospel." (1 Corinthians 9:16 KJV).**

To be relevant in our present day and age, as well as for all of eternity, we must adhere to and adopt the same philosophy, as did Jesus Christ and Apostle Paul. We must recognize various movements and trends in our marketplace and society. We must be willing to embrace change as opportunity instead of fear, without compromising the Gospel. We must approach our "Great Commission" with an empathetic attitude — one of understanding and compassion. We must be where the people are. In today's society the people are flocking to the marketplace and to the Internet. Therefore, it is incumbent upon us, as ambassadors of Jesus Christ, to respond with the purpose of social applicability, practicality and relevance. We strategically choose to be where the people are, in order to exert a positive, significant influence upon them and their condition in this world, as well as in the next. **"And as for me, that utterance may be given unto me, that I may open my mouth boldly, to make known the mystery of the Gospel, For which I am an ambassador in bonds, that therein I may speak boldly, as I ought to speak." (Ephesians 6:19, 20 KJV).**

Ambassadors for Jesus are relevant and our relevance is manifold. We are relevant because the marketplace and the Internet are Almighty God's platforms to reach out with the Gospel of Jesus Christ, connecting the people in our neighborhoods with the people around the world. By appropriately and practically exploiting these venues, we necessarily become our Lord's vanguard — His Line of Conquest — His Army of the Light — His "Conquerors for Christ", from our grassroots commerce centers to the whole of the world, and therefore, relevant to His cause! Because a larger percentage of people, more than ever before in history, are searching spiritually, our practical exploitation of the marketplace and Internet is appropriate. Because God has so blessed us with these marvelous venues from which to proclaim to the world the mighty Name of Jesus — the Name above all names — our sovereign battle cry, our practical exploitation of these platforms is relevant. Because we, as Christians, are commissioned to reach out and convert, and to go into all nations to effect our "Great Commission", our appropriate and practical exploitation of the marketplace and Internet is relevant. **"Go ye therefore, and teach all nations, baptizing them in the Name of the Father, and of the Son, and of the Holy Ghost." (Matthew 28:19 KJV). "...Go ye into all the world, and preach the Gospel to every creature." (Mark 16:15 KJV). "...Thus it is written, and thus it behooved Christ to suffer, and to rise from the dead the third day: And that repentance and remission of sins should be preached in His Name among all nations, beginning at Jerusalem. And ye are witnesses of these things." (Luke 24:46-48 KJV). "Peace be unto you: as My Father hath sent Me, even so send I you." (John 20:21 KJV). "But ye shall receive power, after that the Holy Ghost is come upon you: and ye shall be witnesses unto Me both in Jerusalem, and in all Judea, and in Samaria, and unto the uttermost part of the earth." (Acts 1:8 KJV).**

Just as Jesus and Paul were relevant, so are we! We are appropriate and practical and therefore, relevant to our world. We are practical in our application and preaching of the Gospel and have great bearing on the matters of the day. We demonstrate significance and are highly important to the issues of the world and to the advancement of our Lord's "Great Commission". We have a positive influence in connection with, and have a profound effect on, the times in which we live, and beyond in eternity. In other words, we are relevant in Christ Jesus and His Gospel! Hallelujah! **"Not that we are sufficient of ourselves to think anything of ourselves; but our sufficiency is of God; Who also hath made us able ministers of the New Testament..." (2 Corinthians 3:5,6 KJV).**

These cogent and succinct arguments shall serve us well as we pursue and foster our "Great Commission". Our fellow "Conquerors for Christ" shall embrace the same because they make clear, provide the requisite evidence for and thus, prove "Why Ambassadors for Jesus Christ Are Relevant". I humbly commend to your diligent use in your evangelism and discipleship opportunities and training in the marketplace and beyond, in your daily lives. **"But watch thou in all things, endure afflictions, do the work of an evangelist, make full proof of thy ministry." (2 Timothy 4:5 KJV). "Preach the Word; be instant in season, out of season; reprove, rebuke, exhort with all longsuffering and doctrine." (2 Timothy 4:2 KJV).**

"But they that wait upon the Lord shall renew their strength; they shall mount up with wings as eagles; they shall run, and not be weary; and they shall walk, and not faint." (Isaiah 40:31 KJV).

Declare the Evangel

Our solemn charge in our "Great Commission' is to "Declare the Evangel" to all the world! As Almighty God's own chosen, saved by the Blood of the Lamb, our duty is to advance the love of Christ — His Person — His Truth — His Spirit — His Good News — His Gospel — His Cross — His Resurrection — His Complete and Total Victory — around the world! By virtue of the indwelling and infilling power of the Holy Spirit, we realize the importance of establishing as our purpose the preaching, evangelizing and discipleship of our Lord and Savior Jesus Christ and His Gospel. Just contemplate this for a moment. Due to Father God's eternal, unconditional love for us, He has invited us to commune with Him, through the death, resurrection and ascension of His Son. Through Christ, and in Christ, we are given a vibrant, living, personal relationship with the Godhead through the power of the Holy Spirit. Our personal relationship with our Lord and Savior brings with it our personal commitment and duty to crusade for Jesus Christ with all passion and purpose! Our personal commitment to Jesus Christ is to preach the Gospel to everyone in the world! Our personal commitment to Jesus Christ is to reach out and proclaim the good news and love of "The Evangel" and, by the power of the Holy Spirit, win our fellow men, women and children to an eternal, victorious relationship with Christ Jesus! Thereby, we serve as Christ's ministers of reconciliation, to the glory of God the Father and to the honor of Jesus Christ! Hallelujah! **"And Jesus spake unto them, saying, All power is given unto Me in Heaven and in earth. Go ye therefore, and teach all nations, baptizing them in the name of the Father, and of the Son, and of the Holy Ghost: Teaching them to** observe all things whatsoever I have commanded you: and, lo, I am with you always, even unto the end of the world. Amen." (Matthew 29:19,20 KJV). "But thanks be to God, which giveth us the victory through our Lord Jesus Christ." (1 Corinthians 15:57 KJV). "And all things are of God, who hath reconciled us to Himself by Jesus Christ and hath given to us the ministry of reconciliation." (2 Corinthians 5:18 KJV).

As Almighty God's Saints on earth and Soldiers of the Cross, He has chosen us — commissioned us — in the Army of the Light! Jesus Christ, as Author and Finisher of our faith, is our Commander-in-Chief. He is the Light of the world, the Light of life! His command unto us is to be His voice to all the world! O what an honor! O what a privilege! O how awesome a responsibility! Praise you Almighty God and Father! The world is dying and the Church of Jesus Christ is under siege with the onslaught of the lying enemy. Satan wants to silence the Body of Christ. He has obscured the power of the cross due to the pride of the apostate church. Terrorism is the adversary's latest strategy to intimidate the church and the world. O Saints, O Warriors of Jesus, O Conquerors for Christ, WE ARE THE BODY OF CHRIST! Rise up! Shine with the glory of the Lord! Let us answer God's clarion call to battle! The trump of El Gibor (God our Hero) is sounding! The battle in the heavenlies is raging! Men, women and children are being taken captive and slaughtered by the enemy every day! The time has come to proclaim the TRUTH and make Jesus Christ known from our grassroots commerce centers to the whole of the world! It is time to declare Jesus Christ — the Name above all names! The time has come to demonstrate our violent, active faith in Jesus Christ! O saints, put on the whole Armor of God — the Armor of Light — the Armor of Righteousness — put on the Lord Jesus Christ! Hallelujah! Speak with the Sword of the Spirit! Let us march into battle for Jesus Christ, assert the power of Almighty God and enforce the Victory of the King of kings and Lord of Lords, thereby glorifying His Holy Name and the Throne of God! "Looking unto Jesus the Author and Finisher of our faith..." (Hebrews 12:2 KJV). "I am the Alpha and Omega, the beginning and the ending, saith the Lord, which is, and which was, and which is to come, the Almighty." (Revelation 1:8 KJV).

"Then spake Jesus again unto them, saying, I am the Light of the world: he that followeth Me shall not walk in darkness, but shall have the Light of life." (John 8:12 KJV). "Ye are the light of the world...Let your light so shine before men, that they may see your good works, and glorify your Father which is in Heaven." (Matthew 5:14, 16 KJV). "Arise, shine; for the glory of the Lord is risen upon thee...And the Gentiles shall come to thy light, and kings to the brightness of thy rising." (Isaiah 60:1, 3 KJV). "...The mighty God..." (Isaiah 9:6 KJV). "...[T]he Kingdom of Heaven suffereth violence, and the violent take it by force." (Matthew 11:12 KJV). "...[L]et us put on the armor of light." (Romans 13:12 KJV). "...By the Word of Truth, by the power of God, by the armor of righteousness on the right hand and on the left..." (2 Corinthians 6:7 KJV). "But put ye on the Lord Jesus Christ..." (Romans 13:14 KJV). "Put on the whole armour of God, that ye may be able to stand against the wiles of the devil. For we wrestle not against flesh and blood, but against principalities, against powers, against the rulers of the darkness of this world, against spiritual wickedness in high places. Wherefore take unto you the whole armour of God, that ye may be able to withstand in the evil day, and having done all, to stand. Stand therefore, having your loins girt about with truth, and having on the breastplate of righteousness; And your feet shod with the preparation of the Gospel of peace; Above all, taking the shield of faith, wherewith ye shall be able to quench all the fiery darts of the wicked. And take the helmet of salvation, and the Sword of the Spirit, which is the Word of God: Praying always with all prayer and supplication in the Spirit, and watching thereunto with all perseverance and supplication for all saints; And as for me, that utterance may be given unto me, that I may open my mouth boldly, to make known the mystery of the Gospel, For which I am an ambassador in bonds: that therein I may speak boldly, as I ought to speak." (Ephesians 6:11-20 KJV). "These shall make war with the Lamb, and the Lamb shall overcome them: for He is Lord of lords, and King of kings: and they that are with Him are called, and chosen, and faithful." (Revelation 17:14 KJV).

We have our battlefield — we have our Line of Conquest — O God, thank you for the marketplace and beyond in our daily lives! Let us fully execute our holy commission, and overcome the world as we "Declare the Evangel" — the mighty Name of Jesus Christ! "Give us souls lest we die, that the Lamb who was slain might receive the reward of His suffering, as the glory perfects the unity, and the unity proclaims the glory!" This is our battle cry! May Almighty God bless you as we batter down and through the gates of hell with the Cross of Christ and the preaching of His Gospel, thereby triumphing over the enemy with the Word of God! I commend unto you our "Great Commission" as we "Declare the Evangel" and proclaim the Glory of the risen Lord! Hallelujah! **"But watch thou in all things, endure afflictions, do the work of an evangelist, make full proof of thy ministry." (2 Timothy 4:5 KJV). "And he that overcometh, and keepeth My works unto the end, to him will I give power over the nations." (Revelation 2:26 KJV). "For the preaching of the cross...is the power of God." (1 Corinthians 1:18 KJV). "And I say also unto thee, that thou art Peter, and upon this rock I will build My church; and the gates of hell shall not prevail against it." (Matthew 16:18 KJV). "Now thanks be unto God, which always causeth us to triumph in Christ..." (2 Corinthians 2:14 KJV). "And having spoiled principalities and powers, He made a show of them openly, triumphing over them in it." (Colossians 2:15 KJV). "...Go ye into all the world, and preach the Gospel to every creature." (Mark 16:15 KJV). "And hath made us kings and priests unto God and His Father; to Him be glory and dominion forever and ever. Amen." (Revelation 1:6 KJV).**

> **"But they that wait upon the Lord shall renew their strength; they shall mount up with wings as eagles; they shall run, and not be weary; and they shall walk, and not faint." (Isaiah 40:31 KJV).**

Honor: Our Key to Evangelism & Discipleship

In a previous Message entitled "His Service – The Road Best Traveled", I shared the following:

His service, the Great Commission, commands us to evangelize and witness to as many people as possible, in order to bring them to the end of themselves at the Cross of Christ, in favor of the saving blood of Christ Jesus. When we exercise our freedom in Christ Jesus in favor of the lost and dying men women and children of this world, we love them, as does Jesus. It is the great agape, unconditional, undeserved and sacrificial love with which Christ loves all of mankind — the love that sent Him to the cross. **"If the Son therefore shall make you free, ye shall be free indeed." (John 8:36 KJV)**. **"Hereby perceive we the love of God, because He laid down His life for us: and we ought to lay down our lives for the brethren." (1 John 3:16 KJV)**. **"Herein is love, not that we loved God, but He loved us, and sent His Son to be the propitiation for our sins." (1 John 4:10 KJV)**. By placing Jesus' esteem in the lost and dying people of the world, as well as in our brethren, we honor their potential brilliance and worth in Christ and, at the same time, reinforce the same in ourselves. Indeed, we reap what we sow. **"If there be therefore any consolation in Christ, if any fellowship of the Spirit, if any bowels and mercies, Fulfill ye my joy, that ye be likeminded, having the same love, being of one accord, of one mind. Let nothing be done in strife and vainglory; but in lowliness of mind let each esteem other better than themselves. Look not every man on his own things, but every man also on the things of others. Let this mind be in you, which was also in**

Christ Jesus..." (Philippians 2:1-5 KJV). "Be not deceived; God is not mocked: for whatsoever a man soweth, that shall he also reap." (Galatians 6:7 KJV).

In the Kingdom of God, honor becomes the key to our evangelism and discipleship. When we honor people, we respect them. We hold them in high regard and express care, concern and empathy for their condition. We are careful to consider and communicate their worth at all times in order to build them up and edify them. We demonstrate a particular deference for them. We admire them and revere their individual brilliance, as we place in them the esteem of Jesus Christ. Honor is the condition precedent to establishing a genuine relationship, just as honor is the condition presently necessary to continue, grow and nurture relationships with our fellow men, women and children. When we honor others, in the humility of Christ Jesus, we esteem and exalt them better than ourselves. Hence, honor becomes the key to our evangelism and discipleship. By our consistently and genuinely demonstrating honor, Almighty God magnifies the fruit that said honor bears for His Kingdom in manifold and vast ways! **"But glory, honor, and peace to every man that maketh good, to the Jew first, and also to the Gentile: For there is no respect of persons with God." (Romans 2:10,11). "But the fruit of the Spirit is love, joy, peace, long-suffering, gentleness, goodness, faith, Meekness, temperance: against such there is no law." (Galatians 5:22, 23 KJV).**

Honor is a pivotal leadership principle demonstrated by all great men and women of God. Let us embrace the principles of honor, rather than its antithesis, pride. When we honor one another, we demonstrate Jesus Christ. When we live in pride, we demonstrate the enemy. Pride is being self-centered, as opposed to being other-centered. When one flows in pride, one is incapable of honoring another, even Christ, because you continually exalt yourself, at the expense of Christ and all others. You are the idol of your own life. Pride results in one despising, disparaging, hating, mocking, deriding, vilifying, scorning, ridiculing, criticizing, denigrating, belittling and slandering others. Pride precipitates anger, which in turn causes withdrawal, escalation, invalidation and negative beliefs. There is a great sin that exists in the church today, and that sin is the sin of pride. It is the father of all sin. It is the father of the apostasy! How dare we presume that our wisdom is superior to the infinite wisdom of Almighty God! How dare we exalt ourselves above the Christ — the Messiah — the King of kings, and the Lord of lords! We must kill our pride at the cross every day! Honor emanates from Almighty God. Let us choose honor, to the glory of the Father! Then we do as does Jesus Christ, our Lord, Savior and Role Model. Christ Jesus so honored you and me that He died on the cross for us! Let us choose to honor God, Jesus and Holy Ghost as we honor others, and we shall be blessed with high honor in our relationships. Each and every one of us is created in the image and likeness of God! Let us so honor this miracle! "... [B]ut now the Lord saith, Be it far from Me; for them that honor Me I will honor, and they that despise Me shall be lightly esteemed." (1 Samuel 2:30 KJV). "Woe to the crown of pride..." (Isaiah 28:1 KJV). "I am crucified with Christ: nevertheless I live; yet not I, but Christ liveth in me: and the life which I now live in the flesh I live by the faith of the Son of God, who loved me, and gave Himself for me. (Galatians 2:20 KJV). "These six things doth the Lord hate; yea, seven are an abomination unto Him: A proud look, a lying tongue, and hands that shed innocent blood, A heart that deviseth wicked imaginations, feet that be swift in running to mischief, A false witness that speaketh lies, and he that soweth discord among the brethren." (Proverbs 6:16-19 KJV).

When our honor springs from our relationship with Jesus, it originates of the Father, in Christ, through the Holy Spirit. This is the only legitimate and genuine way to acquire the wherewithal to honor. Anything less is merely false pride. Failure to acknowledge and accept this distinction is the reason so many people live life as a facade, hiding behind masks, so as to live a lie which would be accepted by material, secular, relative, mediocre, societal standards. When these people "honor" each other, it amounts to nothing more than a fraud and a sham — to see how such "honor" will benefit them. Pitifully and sadly, we witness this every day in the church. Let us highly resolve to seek, appropriate and demonstrate true honor — that which emanates from humility — that which is of the God of our Fathers! **"How can you believe, which receive honor** from one another, and seek not the honor that cometh from God only?" (John 5:44 KJV). "Every one that is proud in heart is an abomination to the Lord: though hand join in hand, he shall not be unpunished." (Proverbs 16:5 KJV).**

As Almighty God's "Conquerors for Christ" upon this earth, let us reach out to our fellow men, women and children with consummate honor in order to be the most effective evangelists and disciples for Jesus Christ, as is possible. Our "Great Commission" authorizes us in in the mighty Name of Jesus and orders us from the Throne of God to ..."**Go ye therefore, and teach all nations, baptizing them in the Name of the Father, and of the Son, and of the Holy Ghost." (Matthew 28:19 KJV).** As we transform the church, as well as the marketplace and beyond, in our daily lives, into a prolific platform for Christ, we must ever be vigilant to use said platform to the utmost in honor for one another, and for the lost and dying world, in order to bear fruit for the Kingdom of God, as we are empowered and enabled by the Holy Ghost. The Way to do this is to remain ever humble, yet bold in His service, as we reach out to all men, women and children, in every nation, with the honor which is the essence of Jesus Christ. Let us apply these principles diligently so that no man will be compelled to utter the lament of our Savior. **"I receive no honor from men." (John 5:41).** Let us therefore choose to **"Honor all men. Love the brotherhood. Fear God. Honor the King. (1 Peter 2:17 KJV). "That all men should honor the Son, even as they honor the Father. He that honoreth not the Son honoreth not the Father which sent Him." (John 5:23 KJV).**

Let us come together in one accord and soar as the eagles in Abba's Heavenlies, demonstrating "Honor: Our Key to Evangelism and Discipleship", with the passion and fire of the Holy Spirit in all of our relationships, to the glory of Almighty God. May the Holy Spirit empower and enable us to this end, in the precious Name of Jesus Christ, we pray. Amen.

> **"But they that wait upon the Lord shall renew their strength; they shall mount up with wings as eagles; they shall run, and not be weary; and they shall walk, and not faint." (Isaiah 40:31 KJV).**

Christ Jesus and the Affairs of Men

As long as I can remember, God placed on my heart the burning passion and desire to make a positive, significant difference for mankind. I surmised the most profound way to impact our world would be to serve as President of the United States, arguably the most powerful position on earth today. When I came to know Jesus Christ as my Lord and Savior, my focus began to change as the Holy Spirit quickened me and took over the orchestration of my life. My prayer consistently remains that I may serve Abba, Father and make a significant difference for Jesus Christ in the affairs of men. What has changed is my platform (pulpit), and the means by which to achieve the greatest good possible, to that end. For my part, it is God & Country Revival and The Jesus Brigade, the ministries with which the Lord has blessed me, as well as my business, the Online Christian Webcasting Network. What is your platform (pulpit)? **"And Ezra the scribe stood upon a pulpit of wood...And Ezra opened the book in the sight of all the people...and when he opened it, all the people stood up: And Ezra blessed the Lord, the great God. And all the people answered, Amen, Amen, with lilting up their hands, and worshiped the Lord..." (Nehemiah 8:4-6 KJV).**

The Sword of the Spirit, the spoken Word of God, has a long reach, indeed, and each Christian has been commissioned to spread the Word of God from the grassroots of our neighborhoods to the whole of the world! I respectfully exhort you to seriously and prayerfully reflect on and contemplate this magnificent "Great Commission", with which Jesus Christ has entrusted us, and is inspired by the Holy Spirit. **"...Go ye into all the world, and preach the Gospel** to every creature." (Mark 16:15 KJV). "For the Word of God is quick and powerful, and sharper than any two-edged sword, piercing even to the dividing asunder of soul and spirit, and the joints and marrow, and is a discerner of the thoughts and intents of the heart." (Hebrews 4:12 KJV). "So shall My Word be that goeth out of My mouth: it shall not return unto Me void, but it shall accomplish that which I please, and it shall prosper in the thing whereto I sent it." (Isaiah 55:11 KJV).

We are Father God's present day Ambassadors, Apostles, Prophets, Evangelists, Pastors, Teachers, Saints, Warriors, Soldiers of the Cross of Christ, Ministers, Kings and Priests and "Conquerors for Christ"! We are chosen by Divine Providence to serve as the evangelists and disciples of Jesus Christ! "If any man will come after Me, let him deny himself, and take up his cross daily, and follow Me." Luke 9:23 KJV). "And he that taketh not his cross, and followeth after Me, is not worthy of Me." (Matthew 10:38 KJV). "And whosoever doth not bear his cross, and come after Me, cannot be My disciple." (Luke 14:27 KJV). I know of no more noble purpose on this earth. The Word of God is our weapon as declared in **Revelation 11:5, KJV, "And if any man will hurt them, fire proceedeth out of their mouth, and devoureth their enemies: and if any man will hurt them, he must in this manner be killed."** Who can stand against the Word of God? No one! And our victory is further secured in **Revelation 12:11 KJV, "And they overcame him by the blood of the Lamb, and by the Word of their testimony..."** We are to testify as to what the Word of God has done for us! Hallelujah! His truth shall manifest itself in His time. Woe be it unto them that proudly and boastfully disobey and resist His Word -- it is not an enviable position in which to find oneself. **"Woe unto the inhabitants of the sea coast...the Word of the Lord is against you...I will even destroy thee that there shall be no inhabitant." (Zephaniah 2:5 KJV).**

The earth was created by, and belongs to Almighty God, Christ Jesus and the Holy Ghost. We are His stewards and trustees in our ministries, as well as in the marketplace and beyond, in our daily lives. What ultimately happens lies in the purview of Father God. Enforcing the victory and peace of Christ Jesus and therefore, His significance, can only be realized through the preaching of the saving blood of Jesus Christ and by living and demonstrating His Gospel — Christ and Him crucified and the power of the Resurrection — to the lost and dying world — and to the apostate church. **"But we preach Christ crucified...Christ the power of God, and the wisdom of God." (1 Corinthians1:23, 24 KJV).** Consider the awesome and reverential authority and power our Lord has bestowed upon us to lead the end times revival and restore the church of Jesus Christ! Hallelujah! **"See, I have this day set thee over the nations and over the kingdoms, to root out, and to pull down, and to destroy, and to throw down, to build, and to plant." (Jeremiah 1:10 KJV). "And they that shall be of thee shall build the old waste places: thou shalt raise up the foundations of many generations; and thou shalt be called, The repairer of the breech, The restorer of paths to dwell in." (Isaiah 58:12 KJV). "Behold, I give you power to tread on serpents and scorpions, and over all the power of the enemy: and nothing shall by any means hurt you." (Luke 10:19 KJV).**

I trust the significance of our "Great Commission" is apparent for all of us to passionately and steadfastly embrace the same. Let us execute our commission to our utmost, for the glory of Almighty God and for the honor of Jesus Christ, our Commander-in-Chief! Let us highly resolve to do all that we are empowered and enabled to do, by the power of the Holy Spirit, individually and severally, to ensure that Jesus Christ is the most significant force in the affairs of men. **"For whatsoever is born of God overcometh the world; and this is the victory that overcometh the world, even our faith. Who is he that overcometh the world, but he that believeth that Jesus is the Son of God?" (1 John 5:4,5 KJV). "...Who is the blessed and only Potentate, the King of kings, and Lord of lords..." (1 Timothy 6:15 KJV).**

I am hard pressed to think of a more propitious time in which to serve our Lord and Savior. We are in the last days! Israel has been restored as a nation. Apostasy in the church of Jesus Christ is rampant. Terrorism advances without mercy! Natural catastrophes (earthquakes, hurricanes, tornados, tsunamis, famine) abound. The population of the earth continues to outpace our ability to produce enough food to feed the third world nations — starvations increase, daily. My prayer and expectancy is that our efforts in our ministries, as well as in the marketplace and beyond, in our daily lives, shall prove to be the primary force and platform of Almighty God, which controls the affairs of men, by advancing the Kingdom of Jesus Christ and His Word to every man, woman and child around the world, to hasten the rapture of the church. In order for this to occur we must activate Almighty God's Word! A sheathed Sword is of no value! Therefore, let us draw our Sword of the Spirit out of our scabbards, thus proclaiming the Gospel of Jesus Christ to the world, ever demonstrating our active, violent faith in Jesus Christ! Let us penetrate all aspects of society in every country and nation, from every level of government, to business, to corporate, to universities and colleges, to primary and secondary schools, to the media, to the philanthropists, to all religions, to all social clubs and organizations, et al! I respectfully and earnestly exhort you to do the Work of Jesus Christ! Unsheathe His mighty Sword! Let us dutifully execute our "Great Commission" thereby, reaping God's honor and blessings, in the mighty Name of Jesus Christ. "**...[T]he kingdom of Heaven suffereth violence, and the violent take it bu force." (Matthew 11:12 JKJV). "Preach the Word; be instant in season, out of season; reprove, rebuke, exhort with all longsuffering and doctrine...But watch thou in all things, endure afflictions, do the work of an evangelist, make full roof of thy ministry." (2 Timothy 4:2, 5 KJV). "For the Lord Himself shall descend with a shout, with the voice of an archangel, and with the trump of God: and the dead in Christ shall rise first: Then we which are alive and remain shall be caught up together with them in the clouds, to meet the Lord in the air: and so shall we ever be with the Lord." (1 Thessalonians 4:16, 17 KJV). "And he that overcometh, and keepeth my works unto the end, to him will I give power over the nations." (Revelation 2:26 KJV).**

As we render praise and worship to our God in daily commemoration of His Son's death, burial and Resurrection, let us rejoice and offer thanksgiving for being chosen to serve Him as Commissioned Officers in His Army of the Light! Thank you, O Father God for giving us "Christ Jesus — the Most Significant Force in the Affairs of Men"! Thank you for giving us our ministries, as well as the marketplace and beyond, in our daily lives, to proclaim the Gospel of Jesus Christ to the whole of the world! Thank you for honoring our faithful obedience and for commissioning us to enforce the Victory of Jesus Christ and be overcomers for His great cause! Thank you for anointing us as the "Conquerors for Christ"! Amen! **"Ask of Me, and I shall give thee the heathen for thine inheritance, and the uttermost parts of the earth for thy possession." (Psalm 2:8 KJV). "But thanks be to God which giveth us the victory through our Lord Jesus Christ." (1 Corinthians 15:57 KJV). "Nay, in all these things we are more than conquerors through Him that loved us." (Romans 3:37 KJV).**

"But they that wait upon the Lord shall renew their strength; they shall mount up with wings as eagles; they shall run, and not be weary; and they shall walk, and not faint." (Isaiah 40:31 KJV).

Heroic Spirit of Christ

Let us be ever mindful of the fact that we are moving closer to the rapture of the faithful remnant and the advent of the Second Coming of our Lord and Savior Jesus Christ. **"For the Lord Himself shall descend from Heaven with a shout, with the voice of an archangel, and with the trump of God: and the dead in Christ shall rise first: Then we which are alive and remain shall be caught up together with them in the clouds, to meet the Lord in the air: and so shall we ever be with the Lord." (1 Thessalonians 4:16, 17 KJV).** "And I saw Heaven opened, and behold a white horse; and He that sat upon him was called Faithful and True, and in righteousness He doth judge and make war." (Revelation 19:11 KJV). We are His Sheep — His Children — His Sons and Daughters — His Friends — His Servants — His Stewards — His Soldiers — His Shepherds — His Leaders — His Managers — His Kings — His Priests — His Apostles — His Prophets — His Evangelists — His Pastors — His Teachers — His Conquerors — yes, we are His Disciples! **"And He gave some, apostles; and some, prophets; and some, evangelists; and some, pastors and teachers..." (Ephesians 4:11 KJV).** Praise God that such an honor should be bestowed benevolently upon us — for we are not worthy — but for Christ's saving blood. Christ Jesus is our Lord, our Savior, and our Role Model and Commander-in-Chief! He set the example to which we aspire -- His very character! **"For even hereunto were ye called: because Christ also suffered for us, leaving us an example, that ye should follow His steps." (1 Peter 2:21 KJV).** "But we all, with open face beholding as in a glass the glory of the Lord, are changed into the same image from glory to glory, even as by the Spirit of the Lord." (2 Corinthians 3: 18 KJV). When we live His example by demonstrating His Word, we appropriate our sanctification by being changed into the same image of Christ from glory to glory. Let us take some quiet time to reflect and pray about the price Jesus paid for you and me, in order that we would be saved. **Isaiah 53:3-5 is instructive: "He is despised and rejected of men; a man of sorrows, and acquainted with grief: and we hid as it were our faces from Him; He was despised, and we esteemed Him not. Surely He hath borne our grief, and carried our sorrows: yet we did esteem Him stricken, smitten of God, and afflicted. But He was wounded for our transgressions; He was bruised for our iniquities: the chastisement of our peace was upon Him; and with His stripes we are healed."**

Our Lord was brutalized, despised, rejected, abandoned, scorned, afflicted, stricken, smitten, bruised, wounded and killed — for each one of us. His was the supreme demonstration of unconditional love, compassion and obedience. Jesus Christ is El Gibor, our Hero! "...**The mighty God...**" **(Isaiah 9:6 KJV).** Jesus Christ set the precedent for Christians to follow.

Three specific priorities in our lives come to mind in this context: the first being obedience to Almighty God; the second, a work to do which is advancing our "Great Commission" — and in our case, this involves executing our mission in the secular marketplace and beyond, in our daily lives; and third, His Church — the Body of Christ — to cleanse it from the sin of the apostasy and train up the Army of the Light! **"If you love Me, keep My commandments." (John 14:15 KJV). "Then Jesus said unto them again, Peace be unto you: as My Father hath sent Me, even so send I you." (John 20:21 KJV). "...For the perfecting of the saints, for the work of the ministry, for the edifying of the body of Christ..." (Ephesians 4:12 KJV). "He that followeth after righteousness and mercy findeth life, righteousness, and honor." (Proverbs 21:21 KJV).**

By dutifully executing the aforementioned priorities we please our sovereign God as we lay up treasures for ourselves in heaven by demonstrating the heart, mind and Spirit of Christ Jesus. We are not of this world. We rise above secular humanism, modernistic materialism, relativism and special interest parochialism, in favor of the promise of Jesus' Christocracy — the government of Jesus Christ — a pluralistic society of love, compassion, mercy and justice — where Christ is Supreme Authority — His millennium — His Kingdom of Heaven on earth! How glorious it shall be! **"But lay up for yourselves treasures in heaven, where neither moth nor rust doth corrupt, and where thieves do not break through nor steal: For where your treasure is, there will your heart be also."** (Matthew 6:20,21 KJV). **"And I saw a new Heaven and a new earth: for the first Heaven and the first earth were passed away; and there was no more sea And I John saw the holy city, new Jerusalem, coming down from God out of Heaven, prepared as a bride adorned for her husband."** (Revelation 21:1, 2 KJV).

In our experience, we have discovered that the major weapons the enemy attempts to use to paralyze Christians from realizing the fulfillment of their prophetic destiny are fear and doubt. Jesus is **"The Prince of Peace"**. (Isaiah 9:6). Romans 5:1 declares, **"Therefore being justified by faith, we have peace with God through our Lord Jesus Christ"**. It necessarily follows that fear and doubt are evidence of an unsaved life because they eschew the notion of faith, which is the very essence of Christianity and the condition precedent to peace and reconciliation with God. Scripture is very clear in the regard; **"For God hath not given us a spirit of fear; but of power, and of love, and of a sound mind."** (2 Timothy 1:7 KJV). **"But the fearful, and unbelieving...shall have their part in the lake which burneth with fire and brimstone: which is the second death."** (Revelation 21:8 KJV). We need to hold on to God's promise in **Isaiah 41:10** so that we may overcome these insidious weapons of destruction for all time. **"Fear thou not, for I am with thee: be not dismayed; for I am thy God: I will strengthen thee; yea, I will help thee; yea, I will uphold thee with the right hand of my righteousness."**

Let us highly resolve to seize each and every day for Jesus Christ. Let us demonstrate His holy determination and bravery that we may be worthy to follow Him. The valiant and courageous shall win — we shall enforce His Victory — we shall overcome the enemy! Those who exhibit fear and doubt shall lose! Let us thank the God of our Fathers for His manifold blessings and be witnesses for Jesus Christ by utilizing every means Abba, Father has bestowed upon us. Let us passionately execute our "Great Commission" to its fullest — spreading the Gospel of Christ from the grassroots of our neighborhoods to the whole of the world. Let us establish Christ's line of conquest in the marketplace and around the world! Let us duly execute our individual and several responsibilities so that we may be His kings by conquering the marketplace, thus earning the income necessary to support God's covenant and Church. Let us perform our "Utmost for His Highest" — to the glory of Almighty God! Let us engage the battle as the priests of Jesus Christ in full armor, effectively wielding the sword of the Spirit — the Word of God, as commissioned officers in His Army of the Light! Let us daily proclaim the mighty Name of Jesus Christ as our sovereign battle cry! O saints, let us hold high the Cross of Christ and demonstrate the courage to stand fast and fight along side of our Lord, our Savior, our Commander-in-Chief Jesus Christ, the Son of the living God, thus embodying the "Heroic Spirit of Christ'! Praise God! **"I can do all things through Christ which strengtheneth me." (Philippians 4:13 KJV). "For the preaching of the cross...is the power of God." (1 Corinthians 1:18 KJV). "If any man will come after Me, let Him deny himself, and take up his cross daily, and follow Me." (Luke 9:23 KJV). "And he that taketh not his cross, and followeth after Me, is not worthy of Me." (Matthew 10:38 KJV). "And whosoever doth not bear his cross, and come after Me, cannot be My disciple." (Luke 14:27 KJV). "And hast made us unto our God kings and priests: and we shall reign on the earth." (Revelation 5:10 KJV).**

I exhort you, O "Conquerors for Christ", to do the work of Christ Jesus, so that we may soar as the eagles in God's Heavenlies forevermore! Just as Jesus is our Hero, let the Holy Spirit be the "Wind Beneath our Wings"! May His blessings abound!

"But they that wait upon the Lord shall renew their strength; they shall mount up with wings as eagles; they shall run, and not be weary; and they shall walk, and not faint." (Isaiah 40:31 KJV).

More on Active, Violent Faith

Saints of Almighty God, Jesus Christ is commanding us to share His Gospel. We need to establish a sense of urgency and priority to this end. The need for the realization and ownership of our pursuit of active, violent faith has never been more compelling. Our time is at hand! All prophecy has been fulfilled by Christ Jesus! We must answer the clarion call to win souls to Christ Jesus! Let us be mindful of the words Jesus spoke to Paul in **Acts 26:16, 18; "But rise, and stand upon thy feet: for I have appeared unto thee for this purpose, to make thee a minister and a witness both of these things which thou hast seen, and of those things in the which I will appear unto thee... To open their eyes and to turn them from darkness to light, and from the power of Satan unto God, that they may receive forgiveness of sins, and inheritance among them which are sanctified by faith that is in Me." "...[T]he Kingdom of Heaven suffereth violence, and the violent take it by force." (Matthew 11:12 KJV). "And saying, The time is fulfilled, and the Kingdom of God is at hand: repent ye, and believe the Gospel." (Mark 1:15 KJV).**

As Christians, it becomes our profound duty and obligation to witness on behalf of our Lord and Savior Jesus Christ. We are morally obligated to do so because we have been chosen by Divine Providence to be kings and priests, disciples and evangelists of our Lord. Our glorious burden is that we are indebted by the saving blood of Christ Jesus. We are the executors and trustees of the Gospel of Christ! How compelling is our "Great Commission"! **"I am debtor both to the Greeks, and to the Barbarians; both to the wise, and to the unwise." (Romans 1:14 KJV). "According to the glorious**

Gospel of the blessed God, which was committed to my trust." (1 Timothy 1:11 KJV).

The miracle we are to share is Almighty God's promise of salvation for those who are lost and dying in this world. **John 3:16** declares this promise so completely and vividly; **"For God so loved the world, that He gave His only begotten Son, that whosoever believeth in Him should not perish, but have everlasting life."** How much more are we, God's chosen to be held to the highest of standards in this regard? What level and degree of execution of our active, violent faith does Jesus expect from His elect as His kings and priests on this earth? We are so blessed to be His stewards of the Gospel, which is predestined to reach all corners of this earth to the glory of Jesus Christ! We have been entrusted with the noble and honorable mission of advancing His Gospel to mankind from the grassroots of our neighborhoods to the whole of the world! **"O Timothy, keep that which is committed to thy trust, avoiding profane and vain babblings..." (1 Timothy 6:20 KJV). "All power is given unto Me in the heaven and in earth. Go ye therefore, and teach all nations, baptizing them in the name of the Father, and the Son, and of the Holy Ghost: Teaching them to observe all things whatsoever I have commanded you: and, lo, I am with you always, even unto the end of the world. Amen." (Matthew 28:18-20 KJV).**

My fellow "Conquerors for Christ", the world is rapidly approaching it own destruction. I cite terrorism as the obvious result of the break down of authority and rule of law in society. I refer to the pervasive lack of principles, morality, ethics and righteousness, which is demonstrated day by day in the church and in all nations of the world. From the United States of America — once arguably the strongest bastion of the aforementioned godly traits, to Canada, to Europe, to the Middle East, to the former Soviet Union, to China, to South America, to Africa and the far corners of the earth — Jesus Christ is do desperately needed! **"Now is the judgment of this world: now shall the prince of this world be cast out. And I, if I be lifted up from the earth, will draw all men unto Me." (John 12:31, 32 KJV). "For the Son of man is come to seek and to save that which was lost." (Luke 19:10 KJV).**

It is not enough for us to be saved unto ourselves — we much reach out and convert — indeed, we are so exhorted in **1 Peter 3:15,16, "But sanctify the Lord God in your hearts: and be ready always to give an answer to every man that asketh you a reason of the hope that is in you with meekness and fear: Having a good conscience; that, whereas they speak evil of you, as of evildoers, they may be ashamed that falsely accuse your good conversation in Christ."** My brothers and sisters in Christ, we are to reach out to the dying world with boldness, honor and respect, utilizing the Sword of the Spirit! Praise God! **"But ye shall receive power, after that the Holy Ghost is come upon you: and ye shall be witnesses unto Me both in Jerusalem, and in all Judea, and in Samaria, and unto the uttermost part of the earth." (Acts 1:8 KJV). "...[A]nd take the Sword of the Spirit, which is the Word of God." (Ephesians 6:17 KJV).**

I ask you, can we expect to endure if we forsake the God of our fathers? God has blessed us with much, therefore much is required. My belief is that each Christian has received the imprimatur of Abba, Father, by the shed blood of His Son and, as such, He commands us to advance Christ's mission with Holy Ghost passion — a passion fired by active, violent faith, while tempered with humility and love for others. We are the vanguard chosen by Divine Providence to spread the voice of faith in the pre-eminent Christ Jesus to the world! Our prophetic destiny is to spearhead the search of the truth and to effect a spiritual revolution, revival and renewal of the Cross of Christ worldwide! Praise God! **"...[T]he people that do know their God shall be strong, and do exploits." (Daniel 11:32b KJV). "And He is the Head of the body, the church: who is the beginning, the first-born from the dead; that in all things He might have the pre-eminence. For it pleased the Father that in Him should all fullness dwell." (Colossians 1:18, 19 KJV)." "...[Q]uicken (Revive) Thou me in Thy Way." (Psalm 119:37 KJV). "...[Q]uicken (Revive) me in Thy Righteousness." (Psalm 119:40 KJV). "...[Q]uicken (Revive) Thou me according to Thy Word." (Psalm 119:25 KJV). "...[F]or Thy Word hath quickened (revived) me." (Psalm 119:50 KJV). "For the preaching of the cross...is the power of God." (1 Corinthians 1:18 KJV).**

The question becomes, whether we accept this blessed responsibility? Remember, we shall be held accountable before God for the same! If we are to be sanctified and changed into the image of Christ, then we must act on what we believe is right — we must live with integrity. We must demonstrate and activate our violent faith in Almighty God. Our rendezvous with destiny shall witness the filling of the spiritual vacuum in the world with the knowledge of the glory of the Lord! We battle for the Lord! This battle shall be won by our proclamation of the Gospel of Jesus Christ, and by our demonstrating the unconditional love of Christ toward our fellow men, women and children. Ours shall be a victory of the heart, soul and spirit by the blood and cross of Jesus Christ and the power of His Resurrection! **"For the love of Christ constraineth us; because we thus judge, that if one died for all, then all were dead. And that He died for all, that they which live should not live unto themselves, but unto Him which died for them, and rose again." (2 Corinthians 5:14, 15 KJV). "For the earth shall be filled with the knowledge of the glory of the Lord, as the waters cover the sea." (Habakkuk 2:14 KJV). "... According to your faith be it done unto you." (Matthew 9:29 KJV).**

Our prayer is that we are empowered and enlightened by the Holy Spirit, so that we are filled with the requisite valor and courage to answer Almighty God's clarion call, to be the kings and priests that He has chosen us to be! Our prayer is that we are filled with the grace, authority and power of Jesus Christ's character, mind and Spirit — to be His disciples — and thus overcomers for Him on this earth. Our prayer is that we live for Jesus by building, edifying, loving and nurturing the body of Christ with the Truth of the Word of God within our neighborhoods, while connecting and integrating His Kingdom around the world. To this end, every thought we think, every word we speak and every action we take should reflect Almighty God's grace, love and mercy, while demonstrating boldness, justice, repentance and reconciliation, without fail. **"But God hath revealed them unto us by His Spirit: for the Spirit searcheth all things, yea, the deep things of God. For what man knoweth the things of a man, save the spirit of man which is in him? Even so the things of God knoweth no man, but the Spirit** of God. Now we have received, not the spirit of the world, but the Spirit which is of God; that we might know the things that are freely given to us of God. Which things also we speak, not in the words that man's wisdom teacheth, but which the Holy Ghost teacheth; comparing spiritual things with spiritual. But the natural man receiveth not the things of the Spirit of God: for they are foolishness unto him: neither can he know them, because they are spiritually discerned. But he that is spiritual judgeth all things, yet he himself is judged of no man. For who hath known the mind of the Lord, that he may instruct Him? But we have the mind of Christ." (1 Corinthians 2:10-16 KJV). "... If ye continue in My Word, then are ye My disciples indeed; And ye shall know the Truth, and the Truth shall make you free." (John 9:31,32 KJV).

Ours is a noble mission, which Almighty God is blessing on earth, as He is honoring in heaven. Let us highly resolve to soar with the eagles for the sake of Jesus Christ — for His honor! Let us respectfully invoke the Holy Spirit so that we are successful and significant in this holy quest. We are His kings and priests and I remind you that the literal interpretation of king is — CAN DO! **"I can do all things through Christ which strengtheneth me." (Philippians 4:13 KJV).** What an honorable legacy we shall leave, as we are successful and significant in the eyes of Almighty God. Let us highly resolve to dutifully execute our "Great Commission", on behalf of Christ Jesus. Let us shine with the Light of the Holy Spirit and live in His anointing. Let us boldly demonstrate active, violent faith in our Lord and Savior Jesus Christ! After all is said and done, and we stand before the throne of Christ Jesus, I pray the only words we hear uttered from Lord Jesus shall be; **"Well done, thou good and faithful servant: thou hast been faithful over a few things, I will make thee ruler over many things: enter thou into the joy of the Lord." (Matthew 25:21 KJV).** Let it be written. Let it be done. **"Ye are the light of the world. A city that is set on a hill cannot be hid...Let your light so shine before men, that they may see your good works, and glorify your Father which is in heaven." (Matthew 5:14,16 KJV).**

"But they that wait upon the Lord shall renew their strength; they shall mount up with wings as eagles; they shall run, and not be weary; and they shall walk, and not faint." (Isaiah 40:31 KJV).

Courageous for Christ

"Be strong and of good courage, fear not, nor be afraid of them: for the Lord thy God, He it is that doth go with thee; He will not fail thee or forsake thee." (Deuteronomy 31:6 KJV).

Courage is the quality of being fearless or brave in the face of great danger, difficulty or pain, whether the same is emotionally, physically or spiritually perceived. Courage is a state of mind, purpose and spirit, whereby we effectively overcome whatever challenges us. Courage is valor! As we shall witness in this Message, Almighty God commands us to have courage and to be courageous throughout His Holy Scripture. As you prayerfully read, study and reflect upon this Message, I humbly and earnestly exhort you to contemplate this proposition: Is the courage of the "Conquerors for Christ" the condition precedent to the deliverance of mankind unto the realization of Almighty God's Promise through the Cross of Christ, like unto God's deliverance of the Israelites to the Promised Land from Egypt? **"Be strong and of good courage: for unto this people shalt thou divide for an inheritance the land, which I sware unto their fathers to give them. Only be thou strong and very courageous, that thou mayest observe to do according to all the law, which Moses my servant commanded thee: turn not from it to the right hand or the left, that thou mayest proper whithersoever thou goest." (Joshua 1:6,7 KJV). "But when Jesus heard it, He answered him, saying, Fear not: believe only...." (Luke 8:10 KJV). "For the preaching of the cross...is the power of God." (1 Corinthians 1:18 KJV).**

Courage in one's convictions and beliefs involves demonstrating the same, unconditionally. Hence courage becomes active, violent faith — walking the talk — practicing what you preach, without fear of consequences. Therefore, courage and integrity are inextricably connected, as integrity is entirely dependent upon one's courage. This is because we hold to specific principles and ethics, namely, Holy Scripture. When we demonstrate and live said principles and ethics, we are moral to them. Thus, our morality and our principles and ethics are congruent — they are integral, which means we have integrity — the courage of our convictions and beliefs. **"...[T]he Kingdom of Heaven suffereth violence, and the violent take it by force." (Matthew 11:12 KJV). "Let me be weighed in an even balance that God may know mine integrity." (Job 31:6 KJV). "The Lord shall judge the people: judge me, O Lord according to my righteousness and according to mine integrity that is in me." (Psalm 7:8 KJV). "My little children, let us not love in word, neither in tongue; but in deed and in truth." (1 John 3:18 KJV).**

According to the foregoing arguments, we agree that being courageous means that one possesses and is marked by courage. Also, we are able to agree that courage overcomes all fear, doubt, trepidation, apprehension and hesitation. Moreover, we know that courage does not contemplate escape, retreat or surrender, for these, along with making excuses and blaming others for failure, are the antithesis of courage! Indeed, these are the acts of a coward! The lifeblood of courage is belief in Jesus Christ, obedience to His commandments, along with a "CAN DO" attitude which is His mind! **"Have not I commanded thee? Be strong and of a good courage; be not afraid, neither be thou dismayed: for the LORD thy God is with thee whithersoever thou goest. Whosoever he be that doth rebel against thy commandment, and will not hearken unto thy words in all that thou commandest him, he shall be put to death: only be strong and of good courage." (Joshua 1:9,18 KJV). "And Joshua said unto them, Fear not, nor be dismayed, be strong and of a good courage: for thus shall the Lord do to all your enemies against whom ye fight." (Joshua 10:25 KJV). "Ye are My friends, if ye do whatsoever I command you." (John 15:14**

KJV). "If ye love Me, keep My commandments." (John 14:15 KJV). "I can do all things through Christ which strengtheneth me." (Philippians 4:13 KJV). "But we have the mind of Christ." (1 Corinthians 2:16 KJV).

The courage, which God has chosen all Christians to demonstrate, is the courage of our confidence, conviction and faith in our Lord and Savior Jesus Christ. The courage, which God has chosen all Christians to demonstrate, is the courage to be Jesus Christ's disciples and evangelists. The courage, which God has chosen all Christians to demonstrate, is the courage to be His servant leaders and faithful stewards. The courage, which God has chosen all Christians to demonstrate, is the courage to be His kings and priests. The courage, which God expects those chosen of the marketplace to demonstrate, demands a much higher standard and extends even further. The courage, which God has chosen us to demonstrate, is the courage to do the work of Christ in the secular business world, hence making provision for His vision thus financially supporting His covenant and Church. The courage, which God has chosen us to demonstrate is the courage to pursue our passion and purpose in Jesus Christ, and to spread the Gospel of Jesus Christ from the grassroots of our neighborhoods to the whole of the world, thus growing the body of Christ and hastening the rapture and His second coming. Praise God! "...Have faith in God." (Mark 11:22 KJV). "And David said to Solomon his son, Be strong and of good courage, and do it: fear not, nor be dismayed: for the Lord God, even my God, will be with thee; He will not fail thee, or forsake thee, until thou hast finished all the work for the service of the house of the Lord." (1 Chronicles 28:20 KJV). For God hath not given us the spirit of fear; but of power, and of love, and of a sound mind." (2 Timothy 1:7 KJV).

My colleagues in Christ, I pray that we all embody and demonstrate the courage of God's holy saints upon this earth, thus advancing the "Great Commission" of Christ Jesus. I pray that we are empowered and enabled, through the Holy Spirit, to feed God's sheep spiritually, financially and otherwise. I pray that we are worthy and live up to God's having chosen us to be His commissioned officers in Jesus Christ's Army of the Light in the marketplace and beyond, in our daily lives, thus enforcing His Victory over the adversary. I pray that by engaging God's vision to its fullest, we shall effect a revival and revolution in favor of Jesus Christ and Him crucified and the power of the Resurrection in every corner of the world! This, and much more, is not only possible — it IS the will of the Father — and shall be done by the faithful demonstration of our courage in Jesus Christ. Let us now answer the proposition: Is the courage of the "Conquerors for Christ" the condition precedent to the deliverance of mankind unto the realization of God's Promise through the Cross of Christ, like unto God's deliverance of the Israelites to the Promised Land from Egypt? What say you? What are you doing to ensure that you are "Courageous for Christ" in the great Cause for Christ? I trust that when you face a dangerous situation for Christ that you are being "Courageous for Christ" instead of withdrawing from the same. I trust that when you face a difficult situation for Christ that you are being "Courageous for Christ" instead of withdrawing from the same. I trust that when you face a painful situation for Christ that you are being "Courageous for Christ" instead of withdrawing from the same. I trust that you are being "Courageous for Christ" in the work of Almighty God instead of withdrawing from the same! **"And Jesus came and spake unto them, saying, All power is given unto Me in heaven and in earth. Go ye therefore, and teach all nations, baptizing them in the name of the Father, and of the Son, and of the Holy Ghost: Teaching them to observe all things whatsoever I have commanded you: and, lo, I am with you always, even unto the end of the world. Amen."** (Matthew 28:18-20 KJV). **Fear thou not; for I am with thee: be not dismayed; for I am thy God: I will strengthen thee; yea, I will help thee; yea, I will uphold thee with the right hand of My righteousness."** (Isaiah 41:10 KJV). **"...Fear not; I am the first and the last: I am He that liveth, and was dead; and, behold, I am alive for evermore, Amen: and have the keys of hell and of death." Revelation 1:17, 18 KJV).**

I commend each of you for being "Courageous for Christ" by honoring God's having chosen you to become an integral part of Jesus Christ's Army of the Light by accepting Him as your Lord and Savior. We have thus demonstrated our faithful obedience to His call

— but that was merely our first step — now let us be "Courageous for Christ" as the mighty "Conquerors for Christ" and do the work of Jesus Christ in the marketplace and beyond, in our daily lives, appropriating Almighty God's authority and power each and every day! **"There is no fear in love; but perfect love casteth out fear: because fear hath torment. He that feareth is not made perfect in love." (1 John 4:18 KJV). "And he that overcometh, and keepeth my works unto the end, to him will I give power over the nations." (Revelation 2:26).**

Let us soar as the eagles in God's Heavenlies with all courage, through the saving blood of Jesus Christ, by the power of the Holy Spirit as the "wind beneath our wings." Let it be written. Let it be done. Hallelujah!

"But they that wait upon the Lord shall renew their strength; they shall mount up with wings as eagles; they shall run, and not be weary; and they shall walk, and not faint." (Isaiah 40:31 KJV).

Our Vision/Mission — The "Great Commission"

OUR VISION

"And the LORD answered me, and said, Write the vision, and make it plain upon tables, that he may run that readeth it." (Habakkuk 2:2 KJV). "For the earth shall be filled with the knowledge of the glory of the Lord, as the waters cover the sea." (Habakkuk 2:14 KJV).

OUR MISSION

"And Jesus came and spake unto them, saying, All power is given unto Me in Heaven and in earth. "Go ye therefore, and teach all nations, baptizing them in the name of the Father, and of the Son, and of the Holy Ghost: Teaching them to observe all things whatsoever I have commanded you: and lo, I am with you always, even unto the end of the world. Amen." (Matthew 28:19,20 KJV).

All ye "Conquerors for Christ", Almighty God has chosen us to compelling action in the marketplace and beyond, in our daily lives! God has chosen us to spread the voice of faith in Jesus Christ to the world as His vanguard as chosen by Divine Providence! God has chosen us to launch and sustain the revival the Cross of Christ and the Word of God around the world! God has chosen us to mainstream the moral authority of Holy Scripture and the Gospel of Jesus Christ! God has chosen us to realize and achieve our prophetic destiny to spearhead the search of truth to effect His spiritual revolution, revival and renewal worldwide! God has chosen us to establish ourselves as The Way through which Jesus Christ can flow as rivers of living water in blessing and victory and Resurrection life unto our fellow men, women and children around the world! God has chosen us to provide THE WAY to spread the Gospel to the whole of the world — to every nation — to every human being! God has chosen us to establish and become His Army of the Light, thus creating and maintaining Jesus Christ's line of conquest to the whole of the world! God has chosen us to declare the Name above all names — Jesus Christ — to a lost and dying world! God has chosen us and commands us to be His voice to all the world! God has chosen us to overcome the enemy as we declare the Evangel — the mighty Name of Jesus — as our sovereign battle cry! Is there any doubt that our Vision and Mission are of God Almighty? Who but the Lord God Almighty could conceive such a grand Vision and Mission? Praise God that we are His! Praise God that we are His will! **"And Jesus came and spake unto them, saying, All power is given unto Me in heaven and in earth. Go ye therefore, and teach all nations, baptizing them in the name of the Father, and of the Son, and of the Holy Ghost: Teaching them to observe all things whatsoever I have commanded you: and, lo, I am with you always, even unto the end of the world. Amen." (Matthew 28:18-20 KJV). "Ye have not chosen Me, but I have chosen you, and ordained you, that ye should go and bring forth fruit, and that your fruit should remain: that whatsoever ye shall ask of the Father in My Name, He may give to you." (John 15:16 KJV). "For the preaching of the cross...is the power of God; But we preach Christ crucified...Christ the power of God and the wisdom of God." (1 Corinthians 1:18; 23, 24 KJV). "For I determined not to know any thing among you, save Jesus Christ, and Him crucified." (2 Corinthians 2:2 KJV). "...[Y]ea, woe is unto me, if I preach not the Gospel." (1 Corinthians 9:14 KJV). "For I am not ashamed of the Gospel of Christ: for it is the power of God unto salvation to every one that believeth; to the Jew first, and also to the Greek." (Romans 1:16 KJV). "And I, if I be lifted up from the earth, will draw all men unto Me." (John 12:32 KJV).**

"Jesus saith unto him, I am the way, the truth, and the life; no man cometh unto the Father, but by Me." (John 14:6 KJV).

In order to effect Father God's Vision and Mission in each of us, we must demonstrate TOTAL DEVOTION to Jesus Christ, and when we purpose to be changed into the same image as The Christ, His love shall constrain us to do His work. A half-hearted effort will NOT get the job done. When we demonstrate TOTAL DEVOTION to our Lord and Savior Jesus Christ, God enables us to accomplish our Vision and Mission because His will is always done — we merely need to demonstrate active, violent faith, and God shows us His faithfulness. With Father God and the power of the Holy Ghost, the work of Jesus shall be done. Almighty God has given us sufficient detail about our Vision and Mission that we are able to envision our excellence in Jesus Christ in order to complete this enormous, global task. He has provided us with His direction to follow and execute, for His glory and for the honor of Christ Jesus. Our due diligence and passion in our great Cause for Christ is driven by the excellence of God's Vision and Mission, which He has bestowed upon us. Therefore, in the mighty Name of Jesus Christ, by His blood and cross, and by the power of His Resurrection, we are optimistic and enthusiastic in our holy quest! To this end, we must communicate our Vision and Mission passionately, consistently, and even relentlessly, in order to exhort one other in the work of Jesus Christ. **"And David said to Solomon his son, Be strong and of good courage, and do it: fear not, nor be dismayed: for the LORD God, even my God, will be with thee; he will not fail thee, nor forsake thee, until thou hast finished all the work for the service of the house of the Lord." (1 Chronicles 28:20 KJV). "I will instruct thee and teach thee in the way which thou shalt go: I will guide thee with Mine eye." (Psalm 32:8 KJV). "But we all, with open face beholding as in a glass the glory of the Lord, are changed into the same image from glory to glory, even as by the Spirit of the Lord." (2 Corinthians 3:18 KJV). "For the love of Christ constraineth us; because we thus judge, that if One died for all, then were all dead: And that He died for all, that they which live should not henceforth live unto themselves, but unto Him which died for them, and rose again." (2 Corinthians**

5:14, 15 KJV). "And from the days of John the Baptist until now the Kingdom of Heaven suffereth violence, and the violent take it by force." (Matthew 11:12 KJV).

Our Vision and Mission are rooted in our ethics, principles, values and virtues as found in the Holy Bible, which emanate from the character and love of Jesus Christ. We are the chosen people of Almighty God! Our passion and purpose is our personal relationship in and with Jesus Christ our Lord and Savior, the Lamb of God! **"...Behold the Lamb of God, which taketh away the sin of the world." (John 1:29 KJV).** Our undying quest is to journey "The Road Best Traveled" and making a significant difference for Jesus by convicting and converting as many souls as possible prior to the rapture of the church. While pursuing our passion and purpose, our world becomes a better place for all mankind as we demonstrate Jesus on a daily basis. Thus, our Vision and Mission fulfill the great need of humanity to come to know Jesus Christ as Lord and Savior! This becomes our noble purpose on the earth! The realization of our quest — our great Cause for Christ — requires the DEVOTED participation of all of us. Each TEAM member — the body of Christ — must be consummately dedicated to our Vision and Mission, and must diligently and obediently execute the offices, gifts and anointing with which we are blessed. We are Jesus Christ's warriors, kings, priests, conquerors, servant-leaders, stewards, shepherds, managers, salespersons, orators, writers, apostles, prophets, evangelists, pastors, teachers and disciples, and more. We must complement one another and work in perfect agreement, harmony and unity, as does the Holy Trinity. We must combine our anointing and strengths in order to change the world for Christ. We must believe in our passion, purpose and Cause for Christ, as well as believe in one another. The long-term ramifications of our work involves eternity in Christ Jesus, hence the effects of our work for the salvation of souls through the blood of the Lamb, last forever. **"And the glory which thou gavest Me I have given them; that they may be one, even as We are one: I in them, and Thou in Me, that they may be made perfect in one; and that the world may know that Thou hast sent Me, and hast loved them, as Thou hast loved Me... And I have declared unto them Thy Name, and will** declare it: that the love wherewith Thou hast loved Me may be in them, and I in them." (John 17:22, 23, 26 KJV). "Where there is no vision, the people perish: but he that keepeth the law, happy is he." (Proverbs 29:18 KJV). "Now I beseech you, brethren, by the Name of our Lord Jesus Christ, that ye all speak the same thing, and that there be no divisions among you; but that ye be perfectly joined together in the same mind and in the same judgment." (1 Corinthians 1:10 KJV). "But he that is joined unto the Lord is one spirit." (1 Corinthians 7:17 KJV). "Endeavoring to keep the unity of the Spirit in the bond of peace. There is one body, and one spirit, even as ye are called in one hope of your calling; One Lord, one faith, one baptism, One God and Father of all, who is above all, and through all, and in you all." (Ephesians 4:4-6 KJV).

Fellow Soldiers of the Cross and "Conquerors for Christ", Almighty God is involved in our work, because our work is His work! This "Great Commission" requires our concerted active, violent faith to bring it to fruition. When this happens, we then freely receive the blessings, gifts and grace of Almighty God to finish the work. He is faithful to those Spirit-filled living churches (living organisms) and their brethren who are committed to His Son. Let the Church and her people realize Father God's Vision and Mission — it is up to you and me — it is up to the body of Christ — the Faithful Remnant — the "Conquerors for Christ"! Let us appropriate God's benevolence NOW! Let us assert all of the power of Almighty God against the adversary, sin, false preachers, prophets and teachers in the apostate church, and a lost and dying world, thereby enforcing the Victory of Jesus Christ! The result shall be that we grow the body of Christ — the Army of the Light — the Ecclesia, His church, the called out ones — His Kingdom! **"Jesus answered and said unto them, Verily I say unto you, If ye have faith, and doubt not, ye shall not only do this which is done to the fig tree, but also if ye shall say unto this mountain, Be thou removed, and be thou cast into the sea; it shall be done. And all things, whatsoever ye shall ask in prayer, believing, ye shall receive." (Matthew 21:21,22 KJV). "I am the vine, ye are the branches: He that abideth in Me, and I in him, the same bringeth forth much fruit: for without Me ye can do nothing." (John 15:5 KJV). "The Lord is not slack concerning His promise, as some men count slackness; but is long-suffering to us-ward, not willing that any should parish, but that all should come to repentance...Looking for and hasting unto the coming day of God...And account that the long-suffering of our Lord is salvation..." (2 Peter 3: 9, 12, 15 KJV). "And this Gospel of the Kingdom shall be preached in all the world for a witness unto all nations; and then shall the end come." (Matthew 24:14 KJV).

Should the Vision, Mission and work of Christ in the marketplace and beyond, in our daily lives, give you a sense of being overwhelmed, then praise God. Should the overwhelming aspects of our great Cause for Christ give you pause to ask the question, "Who am I to do this?", then praise God. The very sensation and extent of our feeling overwhelmed is equal to the awesome challenge and, through Jesus Christ, serves as the very spark to ignite the fire of our passion and purpose in our great "Cause for Christ"! Almighty God, the great I AM that I AM, desires us to do Christ's work — and Christ's work derives its legitimacy from the authority of Almighty God! He is with us! We are fulfilling what He wants done! It is time to be faithful in Almighty God! It is time to push to get it done! Let us duly execute "Our Vision/Mission — The "Great Commission!" Praise God! **"And he that overcometh, and keepeth My works unto the end, to him will I give power over the nations." (Revelation 2:26 KJV). "And hath made us kings and priests unto God and his Father; to Him be glory and dominion for ever and ever. Amen." (Revelation 1:6 KJV). "And hast made us unto our God kings and priests: and we shall reign on the earth." (Revelation 5:10 KJV).**

Let us be ever mindful that our diligent preaching and teaching of the Gospel of Jesus Christ, as well as our testimony and witness of our Lord and Savior, are the keys to the Kingdom of Heaven. We are to take authority over the enemy and all of his demons, while proclaiming Jesus Christ to a lost and dying world. **"Study to show thyself approved unto God, a workman that needeth not be ashamed, rightfully dividing the Word of truth." (2 Timothy 2:25 KJV). "Preach the Word: be instant in season, out of season; reprove, rebuke, exhort with all long-suffering and doctrine." (2

Timothy 4:2 KJV). "And they overcame him by the blood of the Lamb, and by the Word of their testimony; and they loved their lives not unto the death." (Revelation 12:11 KJV). "And I will give unto thee the keys of the Kingdom of Heaven: and whatsoever thou shalt bind on earth shall be bound in Heaven: and whatsoever thou shalt loose on earth shall be loosed in Heaven." (Matthew 16:19 KJV). "Behold, I give unto you power to tread on serpents and scorpions, and over all the power of the enemy: and nothing shall by any means hurt you." (Luke 10:19 KJV). As we march on in faithful obedience to our "Great Commission", we fill the earth with the knowledge of the glory of the Lord -- yes, we fill the earth with the Gospel of Jesus Christ -- Who is the perfect manifestation and revelation of the Father! Hallelujah! **"And the Lord answered me, and said Write the vision, and make it plain upon the tables, that he may run that readeth it...For the earth shall be filled with the glory of the Lord, as the waters cover the sea."** (Habakkuk 2:2, 14 KJV).

My colleagues in Christ, let us acquire the daily strength we need to soar as God's eagles in His Heavenlies by living **Isaiah 40:31; "But they that wait upon the Lord shall renew their strength; they shall mount up with wings as eagles; they shall run, and not be weary; and they shall walk, and not faint."**

Commitment, Devotion, Loyalty — All or Nothing

"And He said unto them all, If any man will come after Me, let him deny himself, and take up his cross daily, and follow Me." (Luke 9:23 KJV). "And he that taketh not his cross, and followeth after Me, is not worthy of Me." (Matthew 10:38 KJV). "And whosoever doth not bear his cross, and come after Me, cannot be My disciple." (Luke 14:27 KJV).

It is an incontrovertible truth that our highest priority as "Conquerors for Christ" is to serve Christ with complete commitment, devotion and loyalty. As we daily commemorate our Lord and Savior's sacrificial death, burial and triumphant Resurrection, it is appropriate that we prayerfully reflect upon what is contemplated by the words commitment, devotion and loyalty as applied to each of us, bearing in mind the aforementioned scripture and other relevant scripture.

Let us begin by analyzing the word commitment. To commit means to bind — to pledge — to engage by covenant and promise. Allow me to demonstrate. When we say, "We are committed to Christ", we mean that we covenant and promise to be bound to — to be pledged to — to be engaged with the blood covenant and relational promise in Christ and His Gospel (our sacred honor and purpose). Hence, commitment connotes a continuing obligation and trusteeship to our covenant and promise to demonstrate Christ Jesus and proclaim and witness the Cross of Christ and the power of His Resurrection. **"Commit thy way unto the Lord; trust also in Him;**

and He shall bring it to pass." (Psalm 37:5 KJV). "Who, when He was reviled, reviled not again; when He suffered, He threatened not; but committed Himself to Him that judgeth righteously." (1 Peter 2:23 KJV). "According to the glorious Gospel of the blessed God, which was committed to my trust." (1 Timothy 1:11 KJV). "O Timothy, keep that which was committed to thy trust..." (1 Timothy 6:20 KJV). "For the preaching of the cross... is the power of God." (1 Corinthians 1:18 KJV). "But we preach Christ crucified...Christ the power of God and the wisdom of God." (1 Corinthians1:23, 24 KJV).

To devote oneself means to give up oneself to a person, activity, or sacred cause and purpose. In our experience, devotion contemplates all of these aspects because we are chosen to give up ourselves to a person (Jesus Christ), to vow to live a consecrated, loving yet bold Christian life (activity), and to zealously and ardently advance our "Great Commission" by demonstrating Jesus through our discipleship and by evangelizing Him to the lost and dying world (sacred cause and purpose). **"I beseech thee, O Lord, remember now how I have walked before Thee in truth and with a perfect heart, and have done that which is good in Thy sight." (2 Kings 20:3 and Isaiah 38:3 KJV). "If thou prepare thine heart, and stretch out thine hands towards Him; If iniquity be in thine hand, put it far away, and let not wickedness dwell in thy tabernacles. For then shalt thou lift up thy face without spot; yea, thou shalt not fear." (Job 11:13-15 KJV) "Go ye therefore, and teach all nations, baptizing them in the name of the Father, and of the Son, and of the Holy Ghost." (Matthew 28:19 KJV). "But God forbid that I should glory, save in the cross of our Lord Jesus Christ, by whom the world is crucified unto me, and I unto the world." (Galatians 6:14 KJV).**

Loyalty involves the notion of faithfulness — of being personally devoted to a constituted authority or ideals. By logical extension, loyalty entails the obligation to advance, defend and support our Constituted Authority (Jesus Christ) and His ideals (sacred honor and purpose) through faithful dedication and execution of His Authority — the "Great Commission". **"O Lord God of Abraham, Isaac, and of Israel, our fathers, keep this for ever in the imagi-**

nation of the thoughts of the heart of Thy people, and prepare their heart unto Thee." (1 Chronicles 29:18) "And he said unto them, Go ye into all the world, and preach the gospel to every creature." (Mark 16:15 KJV). "...[A]nd in defense and confirmation of the Gospel." (Philippians 1:7 KJV). "...I am set for the defense of the Gospel." (Philippians 1:17 KJV). "...[T]hat ye should earnestly contend for the faith." (Jude 3 KJV). "These shall make war with the Lamb, and the Lamb shall overcome them: for He is Lord of Lords and King of kings: and they that are with Him are called, and chosen, and faithful." (Revelation 17:14 KJV).

In **Romans 12:1-2**, we are exhorted to offer ourselves as living sacrifices and to transform our minds to the mind of Christ, thus committing ourselves to Him by acknowledging Christ as our leader — our passion — our purpose in life. All of our talents, dreams — yes, our very beings are surrendered to His purpose. We must go back through the Cross of Christ every day and die to self, and live to Christ! **"I am crucified with Christ: nevertheless I live; yet not I, but Christ liveth in me: and the life which I now live in the flesh I live in the faith of the Son of God, who loved me, and gave Himself for me." (Galatians 2:20 KJV).** True success and significance can only be realized through complete and total commitment of our lives to God through Jesus Christ. The more we demonstrate our commitment, the more He will bless us and use us for His glory. God measures our significance by how long the effect of what we do will last. By doing the work of Jesus, the effect of our service we thus render lasts for eternity! **"I beseech you therefore, brethren, by the mercies of God, that ye present your bodies a living sacrifice, holy, acceptable unto God, which is your reasonable service. And be not conformed to this world: but be ye transformed by the renewing of your mind, that ye may prove what is that good, and acceptable, and perfect, will of God." (Romans 12:1-2 KJV).**

Joshua 24:14,15,22, declares that without total devotion to God we commit idolatry. The condition precedent to true devotion is steadfast focus on Jesus Christ and on serving Him — at all cost! It is incumbent upon each of us to exercise constant and eternal vigilance in seeking God's wisdom in maintaining and understanding the high standards of our devotion — and then demonstrating the same at all times. **"Now therefore fear the Lord, and serve Him in sincerity and in truth: and put away the gods which your fathers served on the other side of the flood, and in Egypt; and serve ye the Lord. And if it seem evil unto you to serve the Lord, choose you this day whom ye will serve; whether the gods which your fathers served that were on the other side of the flood, or the gods of the Amorites, in whose land ye dwell: but as for me and my house, we will serve the Lord. And Joshua said unto the people, Ye are witnesses against yourselves that ye have chosen you the Lord, to serve Him. And they said, We are witnesses."** (Joshua 24:14,15,22 KJV). **"Looking unto Jesus the Author and Finisher of our faith; who for the joy that was set before Him endured the cross, despising the shame, and is set down at the right hand of the throne of God."** (Hebrews 12:2 KJV).

Habakkuk 3:17,18, reminds us of the high price of success. Our Lord never said that "The Road Best Traveled" would be easy. We must be loyal and faithful to Jesus and His sacred honor and purpose. As long as our vision, mission, goals and outcomes are properly related to Almighty God, we shall glorify Him and honor Christ. Our loyalty must be unconditional and unidirectional. We must stay the course, at all cost. **"Although the fig tree shall not blossom, neither shall fruit be in the vines; the labor of the olive shall fail, and the fields shall yield no meat; the flock shall be cut off from the fold, and there shall be no herd in the stalls: Yet I will rejoice in the Lord, I will joy in the God of my salvation."** (Habakkuk 3:17, 18 KJV).

John 21:17 directs us to feed Jesus' sheep. There is no release from this commission. What joy we experience in fulfilling the work of Jesus! There is no choice of service in this command. Being of one mind and Spirit with Jesus means that we are of one mind and Spirit with the Father and we are united with the Father and the Son through the Holy Spirit. Once we are committed and take up our cross for Jesus, we dare not turn back. We must demonstrate absolute "Commitment, Devotion and Loyalty" to the opportunity to serve Jesus and to our "Great Commission". These are Christ's terms of discipleship! Hallelujah! **"He saith unto him the third time, Simon, son of Jonah, lovest thou Me? Peter was grieved because He said unto him the third time, Lovest thou Me? And he said unto Him, Lord, Thou knowest all things; Thou knowest that I love Thee. Jesus saith unto him, Feed my sheep."** (John 21:17 KJV). **"And Jesus said unto him, No man, having put his hand to the plough, and looking back, is fit for the kingdom of God."** (Luke 9:62 KJV). **"And he that taketh not his cross, and followeth after Me, is not worthy of Me."** (Matthew 10:38 KJV). **"And whosoever doth not bear his cross, and come after Me, cannot be My disciple."** (Luke 14:27 KJV).

Fellow saints, we have been chosen for high service. We have been committed, bound and pledged by the Divine Authority to our great "Cause for Christ". What high honor and privilege we hold! We have been blessed with Jesus Christ's Vision and Mission, which constitute our long-term course of action to establish Jesus Christ's Line of Conquest in the marketplace and beyond, in our daily lives. To accomplish this, we must give up ourselves in total devotion to Jesus Christ by living a consecrated, loving, yet bold Christian life, while advancing our sacred cause, honor and purpose by witnessing Jesus Christ to the lost and dying world! **"All power is given Me in Heaven and in earth. Go ye therefore, and teach all nations, baptizing them in the Name of the Father, and of the Son, and of the Holy Ghost: teaching them to observe all things whatsoever I have commanded you: and, lo, I am with you always, even unto the end of the world. Amen."** (Matthew 28: 18-20 KJV). We must be faithful and ever loyal to our Constituted Authority, Jesus Christ, by advancing, confirming and defending the "Great Commission"! We owe it to God to be consummately committed, devoted and loyal to the business and ministry with which God has blessed us so that we honor His choice in us, thereby empowering us to **"...[G]o and bring forth fruit..!"** (John 15:16 KJV). **"Ye have not chosen Me, but I have chosen you, and ordained you, that ye should go and bring forth fruit, and that your fruit should remain: that whatsoever ye shall ask of the Father in My Name, He may give it you."** (John 15:16 KJV). **"Ye shall know them by their fruits...by their fruits ye shall know them."** (Matthew 7:16, 20 KJV).

Let us highly resolve to be living sacrifices for Jesus and commend ourselves and our work unto Him. Let us be successful and significant in His eyes by winning souls to eternity. Let us demonstrate total focus on Jesus and exercise eternal vigilance — which is the high standard of our freedom in Christ. Let us live up to the high standards of our devotion each and every day by diligently pursuing our opportunity in Jesus Christ. Let us pay the high price of success as we traverse the "Road Best Traveled". Our Vision, Mission, Goals and Outcomes are properly related to the honor of Almighty God — let us be faithful and loyal to the same. Let us stay the course and feed Jesus Christ's sheep, at all cost, in demonstration of our love for Him. Let us take up our cross and never look back. Let us be of the same mind and Spirit as the Father and the Son. Let us demonstrate absolute "Commitment, Devotion and Loyalty" to Jesus Christ and His/our "Great Commission"! When we do, He shall say to us, **"Well done, thou good and faithful servant." (Matthew 25:21 KJV).** Let us be ever mindful of this incontrovertible truth — with Jesus — it is "ALL OR NOTHING"! Praise God! **"For even hereunto were ye called: because Christ also suffered for us, leaving us an example, that ye should follow his steps: Who did no sin, neither was guile found in His mouth: Who, when He was reviled, reviled not again; when He suffered, He threatened not; but committed Himself to Him that judgeth righteously: Who His own self bare our sins in His own body on the tree, that we, being dead to sins, should live unto righteousness: By whose stripes ye were healed. For Ye were as sheep going astray; but are now returned unto the Shepherd and Bishop of your souls." (1 Peter 2:21-25 KJV).**

My prayer is that each of us truly be "Conquerors for Christ", thus being His kings and priests by demonstrating total "Commitment, Devotion and Loyalty — All or Nothing" for Jesus Christ in the marketplace and beyond, iin our daily lives. Let us, once and for all, live and demonstrate Jesus Christ as our one and only, exclusive PASSION — and to Him be the honor and the glory! **"Nay, in all these things we are more than conquerors through Him that loved us." (Romans 8:37 KJV). "And hath made us kings and priests unto God and his Father; to Him be glory and dominion** for ever and ever. Amen." (Revelation 1:6 KJV). "And hast made us unto our God kings and priests: and we shall reign on the earth." (Revelation 5:10 KJV).

"But they that wait upon the Lord shall renew their strength; they shall mount up with wings as eagles; they shall run, and not be weary; and they shall walk, and not faint." (Isaiah 40:31 KJV).

Whom Shall I Send?

"Also I heard the voice of the Lord, saying, Whom shall I send, and who will go for us?" (Isaiah 6:8a KJV).

I have had the distinct pleasure to meet with Pastor Fletcher Brothers, founder of Freedom Village. The work that Pastor Brothers has been called to do by God, on behalf of our children, is profound. The Victory Singers accompanied Pastor Brothers. What beautiful children of God! It's interesting that, while introducing the Victory Singers, Pastor Brothers indicated that, most likely, eight or nine of them could have perpetrated the crime and pulled the trigger at Littleton, Colorado or Taber, Alberta, at one point in their lives. But, as Pastor Brothers states so well, "They have found the Answer — Jesus Christ our Lord and Savior!" Praise God! **"Therefore being justified by faith we have peace with God through our Lord Jesus Christ." (Romans 5:1 KJV).**

Pastor Brothers exhorted Christians to, "Stop fighting among ourselves doctrinally, denominationally and otherwise, and take up the Cause for Christ to save our children." He said that, "If we don't make it happen, it will happen to us — and already the enemy is killing our children in our schools." **"And grieve not the Holy Spirit of God, whereby ye are sealed unto the day of redemption. Let all bitterness, and wrath, and anger, and clamor, and evil speaking, be put away from you, with all malice: And be ye kind to one another, tenderhearted, forgiving one another, even as God for Christ's sake hath forgiven you." (Ephesians 4:30–32 KJV).**

Pastor Brothers asked how Christians are able to turn away and ignore these ruthless actions of the enemy? He questioned, "What will your answer be to Jesus when He calls you before His Throne and asks you, why did you allow My children to die? Why did you not take action to save My children?" My friends in Christ let us activate our violent faith in Christ to save our children. **"For we must all appear before the judgment seat of Christ; that every one may receive the things done in His body, according to that he hath done, whether it be good or bad." (2 Corinthians 5:10 KJV)**. "...**[T]he Kingdom of Heaven suffereth violence, and the violent take it by force." (Matthew 11:12 KJV). "According to your faith be it done unto you." (Matthew 9:29 KJV)**.

Father God also blessed me by allowing me to be part of history in working with Dr. Jerry Falwell. God's timing is always perfect when you obey Him. **"(For not the hearers of the law are just before God, but the doers of the law shall be justified)." (Romans 2:13 KJV)**. I was privileged to attend a Sunday service at Thomas Road Baptist Church, which was founded by Dr. Falwell 40 years ago. It is a beautiful place of worship as it was designed by Thomas Jefferson. Dr. Falwell abandoned his prepared sermon and shared his thoughts regarding the Littleton, Colorado massacre. It was then that Dr. Falwell issued a " Call to Action" for Christians to "Take America Back for Jesus". It was all very moving and electrifying. We could sense the Holy Spirit's presence as the congregation responded with open arms at the "Call to Action". **"Wherefore also we pray for you, that our God would count you worthy of this calling, and fulfill all the good pleasure of His goodness and the work of faith and power." (2 Thessalonians 1:11 KJV)**.

Two days later we filmed my interview with Dr. Falwell. We spent the entire day in Dr. Falwell's studio on the campus of Liberty University. (By the way, Pastor Fletcher Brothers' son attended Liberty University). While our taping was completed in only one take — the Holy Spirit always moves when we need and rely on Him — we engaged the balance of the day fleshing out God's Vision for Dr. Falwell's "Call to Action". By virtue of our being present, Dr. Falwell's "Call to Action" was expanded to include Canada, as well. Bear in mind that this was prior to the tragic incident in Taber,

Alberta! Soon this "Call to Action" shall spread to the world – at – large! To God be all the glory! " **...[Y]ea I have spoken it, I will also bring it to pass, I have purposed it, I will do it." (Isaiah 46:11 KJV).**

Our time with Dr. Falwell and his faithful afforded us the opportunity to demonstrate our "Commitment, Devotion and Loyalty" to Jesus and His great cause in the marketplace and beyond, in our daily lives. Through our professionalism we established great credibility with a co-laborer and leader for God and his highly effective team. Our relationship can only grow more synergistically into the future as we pursue God's Vision to take America, Canada and the world back for Jesus! **"And the LORD answered me, and said, Write the vision, and make it plain upon the tables, that he may run that readeth it." (Habakkuk 2:2 KJV).**

Saints, if we fail to do the work of Jesus, then what? Have you ever been persecuted for sharing your faith in Christ? Has your faith cost you anything? If not, perhaps you had better re-examine your faith to see if it measures up to the One who said, **'Blessed are ye when men shall revile you, and persecute you, and say all manner of evil against you falsely, for My sake. For so persecuted they the prophets which were before you.' (Matthew 5:11 KJV)."**

Pray tell, if a terrorist held a gun to your face and asked you, "Do you believe in God?" What would your answer be? Can you imagine yourself, your son, your daughter, your spouse, your mother, your father, you sister, your brother your grandchildren, any extended member of your family or friends being placed in this position? My dear Saints, this did happen, and it is happening via the ruthless actions of the terrorists all over the world! When it does happen, it happens to each one of us because, as Christians, we are all members of one family — the body of Christ — His church — His Kingdom! Who among us shall take up the bloodstained torch of God's love in Christ that these precious students of tender years demonstrated? Who among us will take up Christ's cross and follow Him? **"Then Jesus said to His disciples, If any man will come after Me, let him deny himself, and take up his cross, and follow Me." (Matthew 16:24 KJV).**

My fellow "Conquerors for Christ", we are poised to make a significant difference for Jesus. These tragic events have raised the consciousness and driven home the NEED for Jesus Christ. Who among us will step out in faith and stand with Christ on behalf of our children? Who among us would ignore or retreat from God's clarion "Call to Action" to take America, Canada and the world back for Jesus? Who among us is outraged by the willful, wanton, premeditated, heinous slaughter of our children in America, Canada, and the world at large? Who among us possesses the requisite righteous indignation, as a result of Jesus Christ being legislated, regulated and adjudicated out of the public square and our schools — even out of the affairs of men. Who among us is sickened by the counterculture, media, Hollywood, and the like, the pervasive violence, hate and dehumanizing aspects of video games, and the Internet underground, et al? Who among us desires to take America back for Jesus? Who among us desires to take Canada back for Jesus? Who among us desires to take the world back for Jesus? Who among us is willing to pay the price and do the work necessary to accomplish these desires — which is our responsibility in Christ Jesus? **"For I am determined not to know anything among you, save Jesus Christ, and Him crucified."** (1 Corinthians 2:2 KJV). **"And whatsoever ye do, do it heartily, as to the Lord, and not unto man; knowing that of the Lord ye shall receive the reward of the inheritance: for ye serve the Lord Christ."** (Colossians 3:23-24 KJV).

What would your answer be? Who among us shall choose to make a difference for Jesus Christ and our children? Who among us shall demonstrate their active, violent faith in Jesus Christ? Let each of us determine to actively evangelize, disciple and propagate the "Cause for Christ" to America, Canada and the World! Let us activate our violent faith for Christ and the children! Why do we tarry? O God, give us the will, the courage, the need to act! O God have me overcome my fears and complacency! **"...[T]he Kingdom of Heaven suffereth violence, and the violent take it by force."** (Matthew 11:12 KJV). **"For God hath not given us a spirit of fear; but of power, and of love, and of a sound mind."** (2 Timothy 1:7 KJV). **"Fear thou not; for I am with thee: be not dismayed, for I am thy God. I will strengthen thee; yea, I will help thee;**

yea, I will uphold thee with the right hand of My righteousness." (Isaiah 41:10 KJV).

If we fail to respond — if we choose not to act — if we miss this opportunity to do the work — may God have mercy on our souls! Who among us will allow these innocent to have died in vain? Who among us will turn our back on Jesus? **"And Jesus said unto him, No man having put his hand to the plough and looking back, is fit for the Kingdom of God." (Luke 9:62 KJV).**

Soldiers of Jesus Christ, God has chosen us to high service. Our responsibility is to properly and effectively steward and release the power of God's gifts, for His glory. Our responsibility is to evangelize and shepherd His flock around the world, from the grassroots of our neighborhoods to the whole of the world. Our domain is the marketplace and beyond, in our daily lives. Our responsibility is to BE the servant leaders of Jesus Christ. Our responsibility is to STAND and FIGHT side by side with our Commander-in-Chief, our Lord and Savior Jesus Christ. Who among us stands ready? **'Wherefore take unto you the whole armor of God, that ye may be able to withstand in the evil day, and having done all, to stand." (Ephesians 6:13 KJV). "And he that overcometh, and keepeth My works unto the end, to him I will give power over the nations." (Revelation 2:26 KJV).**

Let us choose to activate our violent faith! Let us choose to do the work of Jesus Christ! Let us choose to demonstrate our faith with our works! Once we are saved, God expects us — in fact He commands us — to not be hearers of the Word only, but doers as well. Works when we are in Christ, are an extension of Christ's ministry. In fact, works are not ends in themselves, but they demonstrate God's love toward others so that they will know God loves them and so they will desire to learn about God's provision for their needs. The Bible says a man is not helped if we pass by him, wish him well, and tell him of God's love. No, God's love is demonstrated by attending to the man's physical needs and helping him out of the ditch. This is how people learn that the Father has sent the Son. Works must never replace faith and the sharing of the Gospel, but they are a natural extension of the same. **"Arise, shine; for thy light is come, and the glory of the Lord is risen upon thee. For , behold, the dark-**

ness shall cover the earth, and gross darkness the people: but the Lord shall arise upon thee, and His glory shall be seen upon thee. And the Gentiles shall come to thy light, and the kings to the brightness of thy rising." (Isaiah 60:1-3 KJV).** "Let your light so shine before men, that they may see your good works, and glorify your Father which is in heaven." (Matthew 5:16)."

Who will take up the torch of Jesus Christ? Who will show the world that Jesus Christ is "**... [T]he Way, the Truth and the Life"? (John 14:6 KJV).** Who will exercise their freedom in Jesus Christ and demonstrate "Valor In Humility" and "Leadership — Showing The Way" by His example, to guide, exhort, direct by influence and persuade the world that Jesus is the only Way to Heaven? "**...[N]o man cometh unto the Father, but by Me." (John 14:6 KJV).** Who will demonstrate the "Character of Jesus Christ" by being "Shepherds for Christ" and "Architects of Heroes for Christ" and take up His torch and win the world back for Him? Who will give their total "Commitment, Devotion and Loyalty" — their "All or Nothing" for Jesus Christ and our fellow men, women and children? Who will activate their violent faith, proving that "Christ's Character is Our Destiny" and take the world back for Jesus Christ? Who will embrace the "Heroic Spirit of Christ" and be His disciple and evangelist? Who will assure that Jesus Christ is the most significant aspect in the "Affairs of Men"? Who will show and live "Honor: Our Key to Discipleship" toward the lost and dying world? Who will demonstrate "Why Jesus Christ IS Relevant" and appropriate in the affairs of men? Who will engage the "Great Commission" to "Declare the Evangel"? Who will be in "His Service — The Road Best Traveled" and "**...[D]eny himself and take up his cross daily, and follow Me"? (Luke 9:23 KJV).** Who will demonstrate "Faithful Obedience" to Jesus and respond appropriately to His choice in them to be His Servants, Stewards, Shepherds and Soldiers? Who will exercise "Responsibility to Jesus" — " Our Most Significant Responsibility"? Who will achieve their "Greatest Destiny and Highest Nobility" for Jesus Christ? Who will pursue God's "Vision, Goals" and exercise the "Positive Self-Discipline" to accomplish the same, in Jesus' mighty Name? Who will change the world by exhorting others to being "Crucified with Christ & Changed into His

Image" for our Lord and Savior Jesus Christ? Who will "Walk the Talk - - through "Integrity in Christ"? Who will proclaim the Name above all names to the lost and dying world? Who will advance the "Great Commission" of our Lord and Savior Jesus Christ thus being "Courageous for Christ?" **"And Jesus came and spoke unto them saying, All power is given unto Me in heaven and in earth. Go ye therefore, and teach all Nations, baptizing them in the name of the Father, and of the Son, and of the Holy Ghost: Teaching them to observe all things whatsoever I have commanded you: and, lo I am with you always, even unto the end of the world. Amen." (Matthew 28:18-20 KJV).**

Let us be empowered and enabled once and for all to do the work of Jesus Christ. Let us be His kings and priests. Let us shine with His light — with the brilliance of the Holy Spirit, Himself. **"Ye are the light of the world. A city that is set on a hill cannot be hid. Let your light so shine before man, that they may see your good works, and glorify your Father which is in heaven." (Matthew 5:14,16 KJV).** When we demonstrate Jesus — when we save our children — when we save our countries — when we save our world — when we have obeyed His command to **"Feed My Sheep"** according to John 21:17, then He shall say, **"Well done, thou good and faithful servant." (Matthew 25:21 KJV).** What say ye? What is your answer? Let us live Jesus Christ. Let us honor His choice in us. Let us bring forth the harvest. Let us bring forth the fruit. **"Ye have not chosen Me, but I have chosen you and ordained you, that ye should go and bring forth fruit, and that your fruit should remain; that whatsoever ye shall ask of the Father in My name, He may give it you." (John 15:16 KJV).**

Praise God for Jesus Christ! Praise God for the Holy Spirit! Praise God for His Church, the body of Christ! Praise God for our families and children! Praise God for our countries! Praise God for the world. Praise God for the saving blood of Jesus Christ! Praise God for the example of Jesus Christ! Praise God for the courage, strength and grace to BE JESUS, and do His work! **"For even hereunto were ye called: because Christ also suffered for us, leaving us an example, that ye should follow His steps: Who did no sin, neither was guile found in His mouth: Who, when He was** reviled, reviled not again; when He suffered, He threatened not; but committed Himself to Him that judgeth righteously: Who His own self bare our sins in His own body on the tree, that we, being dead to sins, should live unto righteousness: By whose stripes ye were healed. For Ye were as sheep going astray; but are now returned unto the Shepherd and Bishop of your souls." (1 Peter 2:21-25 KJV). "...[B]ut a doer of the work, this man shall be blessed in His deed." (James 1:25 KJV).

My prayer is that each of us truly seize the day for Jesus and be His kings and priests by demonstrating total "Commitment, Devotion and Loyalty". Let us spearhead the battle to take the world back for Jesus! Let us once and for all live and demonstrate Jesus Christ as our one and only, exclusive PASSION and PURPOSE! And to Him be the glory! **"And hath made us kings and priests unto God and his Father; to Him be glory and dominion for ever and ever. Amen". (Revelation 1:6 KJV).**

Let us praise God for His abundant blessings as He continues to prepare us to spearhead the battle for winning America, Canada and the world back for Jesus. As God's kings and priests on this earth, it is incumbent upon us to conquer the marketplace by fostering holiness and living according to biblical principles. It is our sacred duty to proclaim Jesus Christ to the lost and dying world by demonstrating Jesus Christ with boldness and passion. Let us activate our leadership in the affairs of men by demonstrating that Jesus Christ is the most significant aspect in the affairs of this world. Let us demonstrate our obedience to God through our active, violent faith! Let us take the world back for our children and grandchildren for the sake of Jesus Christ! **"And I thank Christ Jesus our Lord, who hath enabled me, for that He counted me faithful..." (1 Timothy 1:12 KJV).** "... [B]ut a doer of the work, this man shall be blessed in his deed." (James 1:25 KJV).

Let us answer Almighty God's clarion call with the following response; **"Also I heard the voice of the Lord, saying, Whom shall I send, and who will go for us? Then said I, Here am I; send me." (Isaiah 6:8 KJV)**

"But they that wait upon the Lord shall renew their strength; they shall mount up with wings as eagles; they shall run, and not be weary; and they shall walk, and not faint." (Isaiah 40:31 KJV).

Architects of Heroes for Christ

My definition of Hero is comprehensive and manifold. In my mind, a Hero is an individual who demonstrates persistent strength, resolve, endurance and courage in the face of tremendous adversity, danger and travail. A Hero is committed and dedicated to the undying quest of doing honorable deeds and works, as a humble servant of all. A Hero is a loyal and devoted friend with a pure and uncompromising heart whom one can trust as an ally and reliable confidant. A Hero lives with great integrity and veracity whose actions are consistent with words that are spoken. A Hero knows, loves, respects and reveres all people, unconditionally, and places the esteem of Jesus Christ in each and every individual. A Hero speaks and acts humbly yet boldly on behalf of truth, being faithful and obedient to the same, at all times. A Hero is a responsible steward and soldier who eschews self-interest in favor of a noble cause and great destiny. A Hero positively influences humanity with high purpose and passion. A Hero seeks to be successful and significant in the eyes of Almighty God and cares not what the secular, humanistic and materialistic society-at-large may think, say, or do. A Hero is a transforming, persevering leader of consequence who possesses exemplary character and seeks to empower others to carry on the lofty principles of discipline and responsibility, who will take care to grow and nurture the spirit of the body (esprit de corps). A Hero is willing to sacrifice everything — status, possessions, reputation, even life itself — for the sake of Almighty God and His people. Saints, my definition of Hero is our Lord and Savior Jesus Christ! **"...The mighty God..." (Isaiah 9:6 KJV). "I am crucified with Christ: nevertheless I live; yet not I, but Christ liveth in me: and** the life which I now live in the flesh I live by the faith of the Son of God, who loved me, and gave himself for me." (Galatians 2:20 KJV). "Greater love hath no man than this, that a man lay down his life for his friends." (John 15:13 KJV).

My friends, our sense of duty in Christ can only be realized by our sense of the heroic — our sense of Jesus Christ, Himself. We are chosen to seek and aspire to the very mind, heart and spirit of our Hero, Jesus Christ. By prayerful, diligent and passionate pursuit of our Hero, we are thus empowered to be His disciples on this earth. **"For whom He did foreknow, He also did predestinate to be conformed to the image of His Son..." (Romans 8:29 KJV).** By growing and nurturing the spirit of the body (esprit de corps) we become the powerful, synergistic organism — the Body of Christ — upon this earth, whose commission is to convert and disciple our fellow men, women, and children around the whole of the world. Each of us is a vital part of the whole body of Christ. Each of us is integral to and must complement our Lord's "Great Commission". This is our sense of duty — our very reason for living, as God's kings and priests for the kingdom! **"And hast made us unto our God kings and priests: and we shall reign on the earth." (Revelation 5:10 KJV). "Go ye therefore and teach all nations, baptizing them in the name of the Father, and of the Son, and of the Holy Ghost: Teaching them to observe all things whatsoever I have commanded you: and, lo, I am with you always, even unto the end of the world. Amen." (Matthew 28:19,20 KJV).**

Embracing Christ as our Hero means being His friend. **In John 15:14, 15, Jesus says, "Ye are My friends, if ye do whatsoever I command you. Henceforth I call you not servants; for the servant knoweth not what his lord doeth: but I have called you friends; for all things that I have heard of My Father I have made known unto you."** My friends, each of us is a necessary and privileged part of Jesus' inner circle. Jesus confides in us the truths of our God and Father. Our sense of the heroic demands that we are loyal to Christ — and to each other — as His church and body here on this earth. The very honor of our Lord and Savior is at stake in our earthly, bodily lives! How do we measure up in this regard? True friends in Christ live and demonstrate the character of Christ, in good times and through trials and tribulations. **"A friend loveth at all times, and a brother is born for adversity." (Proverbs 17:17 KJV).** A friend in Christ — a Hero for Christ — has complete and resolute trust, faith and obedience, in Jesus Christ. **"And the scripture was fulfilled which saith, Abraham believed God, and it was imputed unto Him for righteousness: and he was called the Friend of God." (James 2:23 KJV).**

My friends in Christ, God has chosen us unto high service. He has chosen us to demonstrate Jesus Christ, at all cost. Do we truly possess a pure and uncompromising heart — the heart and mind of Christ? Are we willing to give it all up for the sake of Christ — our homes, cars, boats, reputation, money, clothes, TV's, computers, beds — even our lives? Do we have Jesus' agenda in our hearts — or do we have our own agenda — and convince ourselves it is His? Are we so in love with Jesus that we seek to do His will, exclusively? Let us consider the fact that we are mortal — we shall physically die and leave this world — what can we take with us but our heroism for Christ? Let us know and demonstrate God's gift of faith, in Jesus' mighty Name. Let us live up to His choice in us as His Heroes on this earth! **"Ye have not chosen Me, but I have chosen you, and ordained you, that ye should go and bring forth fruit, and that your fruit should remain: that whatsoever ye shall ask of the Father in My name, He may give it you. These things I have commanded you, that ye love one another." (John 15:16,17 KJV). "These shall make war with the Lamb, and the Lamb shall overcome them: for He is Lord of lords, and King of Kings: and they that are with Him are called, and chosen, and faithful." (Revelation 17:14 KJV).**

Let us pray that we muster the wherewithal to enforce the victory of the cross and Resurrection, and be Christ's Heroes — His mighty men and women who deliver and demonstrate His holy Gospel at home, in church and in the marketplace. Just as David depended on his mighty men, let us have Jesus depend upon each and every one of us as the "Conquerors for Christ". **"These be the names of the mighty men whom David had..." (2 Samuel 23:8 KJV).** Let your name and my name be included among the mighty men and women of Jesus Christ, our Commander-in-Chief! Let us answer

God's clarion call to service as did Isaiah in **Isaiah 6:8, "Also I heard the voice of the Lord, saying, Whom shall I send, and who will go for us? Then said I, Here am I; send me."**

My friends in Christ, recent polls show that our decline in morality is a major concern of adults in North America. This decline in morality has precipitated the perpetration of violent crimes by our youth, as well as terrorism and the result is the spiraling of our society downward into a terrifying, evil manifestation of the enemy's plan. There is only one way in which we can extricate the world from the captivity of Satan — and our answer is The Way, Himself — by the saving blood of our Lord and Savior Jesus Christ! **"I am the Way, the Truth and the Life: no man cometh unto the Father, but by Me." (John 14:6 KJV).** Our time has come for our pastors to preach the Cross of Jesus Christ with great boldness and passion, and it is our duty to exhort them to such active, violent faith — thus being Heroes for Christ. Our time has come for each and every member of the body of Christ to declare the Evangel — to convert souls to Christ — and then disciple these precious souls, as Jesus commands — thus being Heroes for Christ. As God's kings and priests, whose passion is to raise income to support His covenant and Church and to save souls for Christ, we must assume this responsibility and make it as crucial to our existence as the air we breathe! **"...[T]he Kingdom of Heaven suffereth violence, and the violent take it by force." (Matthew 11:12 KJV).** Remember our time in this world is brief and fleeting. Our time subsequent to this world is for eternity. Do you stand ready to take up your cross for Jesus and forsake the pleasures and comforts of this life — or not? **Yea doubtless, and I count all things but loss for the exellency of the knowledge of Christ Jesus my Lord: for whom I have suffered the loss of all things, and do count them but dung, that I may win Christ." (Philippians 3:8 KJV).** "Whosoever will come after Me, let him deny himself and take up his cross, and follow Me." (Mark 8:34 KJV). "...Woe is unto me, if I preach not the Gospel!" (1 Corinthians 9:16 KJV).

My friends, let us now, forevermore, cast aside every weight and sin (pride, fear, doubt, selfishness, lies, lack of courage, lack of faith, worry, being comfortable according to secular standards, et al) and do the work of Jesus Christ. Remember what Jesus endured for us -- this should give us some perspective of how unworthy we truly are. But for the saving blood of Jesus Christ — there go I. Saints, let us activate our commissions in Jesus' Army of the Light. Let us return from being AWOL (Absent With Out Leave). Let us eschew and overcome the treason and mutiny against our Lord and Savior Jesus Christ! Let us remember what He did for us and reciprocate with our valiant execution of our "Great Commission"! Only by being Heroes for Christ will we be able to show our children and grandchildren how to do the same — thus becoming "Architects of Heroes for Christ." Praise God! **"Wherefore seeing we also are compassed about with so great a cloud of witness, let us lay aside every weight, and the sin which doth so easily beset us, and let us run with patience the race that is set before us, Looking unto Jesus the Author and Finisher of our faith; who for the joy that was set before Him endured the cross, despising the shame, and is set down at the right hand of the throne of God." (Hebrews 12:1,2 KJV).**

Let us be mindful of the fact that America and Canada were founded by Christian men and women. Indeed, the very foundations of these countries are based upon the Bible. The question becomes, what legacy shall we leave regarding our freedom — even our freedom in Christ? Our forefathers were great Heroes for Christ — shall we take up their torch of courage and faith and be Heroes for Christ, as well? Let us pray to God, in Jesus Name, that we do! **"I press toward the mark for the prize of the high calling of God in Christ Jesus." (Philippians 3:4 KJV). "And ye shall know the truth, and the truth shall make you free." (John 9:32 KJV). "I can do all things through Christ which strengtheneth me." (Philippians 4:13 KJV). "Nay, in all these things we are more than conquerors through Him that loved us." (Romans 8:37 KJV).**

> **"But they that wait upon the Lord shall renew their strength; they shall mount up with wings as eagles; they shall run, and not be weary; and they shall walk, and not faint." (Isaiah 40:31 KJV).**

Shepherds for Christ

"I am the Good Shepherd: the Good Shepherd giveth His life for the sheep. I am the Good Shepherd, and know My sheep, and am known of Mine. As the Father knoweth Me, even so know I the Father: and I lay down My life for the sheep. And other sheep, I have, which are not of this fold: them also I must bring, and they shall hear My voice; and there shall be one fold, and One Shepherd." (John 10:11,14,15,16 KJV).

"Shepherd" is a fascinating word to contemplate. Indeed, "shepherd" embodies the very characteristics of our Lord and Savior, Jesus Christ. Let us carefully examine the word "shepherd" in the context of Christ Jesus so that we may clearly perceive and discern our "Role Model" and what we are to do in the marketplace and beyond, in our daily lives. A "shepherd" is a person who leads, directs, governs, guides and shows the way. A "shepherd" tends, takes care of, serves, ministers, and looks after his flock. A "shepherd" herds and gathers together and closely watches over his flock. A "shepherd" guards, defends, protects and keeps safe from harms way his flock. A "shepherd" lays down his life for his flock. **"For unto us a child is born, unto us a Son is given: and the government shall be upon His shoulder...Of the increase of His government and peace there shall be no end...The zeal of the Lord of hosts shall perform this." (Isaiah 9:6, 7 KJV). "The Lord is my Shepherd, I shall not want. He maketh me to lie down in green pastures: He restoreth my soul: He leadeth me in the paths of righteousness for His Name's sake. Yea, though**

I walk through the valley of the shadow of death, I will fear no evil: for thou art with me; Thy rod and Thy staff they comfort me. Thou preparest a table before me in the presence of mine enemies: Thou anointest my head with oil; my cup runneth over. Surely goodness and mercy shall follow me all the days of my life: and I will dwell in the house of the Lord forever." (Psalm 23 KJV). "I am the Good Shepherd: the Good Shepherd giveth His life for the sheep." (John 10:11 KJV).**

    We can all agree that "shepherd" is a most powerful and profound word. What a marvelous and vivid picture it paints! Who among us are able to honestly identify as "Shepherds for Christ"? Do we as Christians, purchased by the blood of Jesus Christ, live and demonstrate the characteristics of being a "shepherd" — of being Christ? Our goal here on earth is to aspire to the same mind and heart of Jesus — to pursue excellence in the essence of Christ — to be changed into His image from glory to glory! Hallelujah! **"Now the Lord is that Spirit: and where the Spirit of the Lord is, there is liberty. But we all, with open face beholding as in a glass the glory of the Lord, are changed into the same image from glory to glory, even as by the Spirit of the Lord." (2 Corinthians 3:17, 18 KJV).** Do we consciously and diligently carry out our "Great Commission" each and every day in the marketplace and beyond, in our daily lives? Do we evangelize Jesus Christ to the lost and dying world? Do we disciple and "shepherd" our fellow men, women and children in Christ? There are so few laborers for the Kingdom. There are so few laborers to gather to His scattered sheep. There are so few laborers for the harvest of souls. **"But when He saw the multitudes, He was moved with compassion on them, because they fainted, and were scattered abroad, as sheep having no shepherd. Then saith He unto His disciples, The harvest truly is plenteous, but the laborers are few; Pray ye therefore the Lord of the harvest, that He will send forth laborers unto His harvest." (Matthew 9:36-38 KJV).**

    If we are not serving as Christ's good "shepherds", then what has become of us? What is the alternative? Are we bad "shepherds"? What if we are merely apathetic, "idol" (idle) and indifferent to our "Great Commission"? God answers us very directly in **Zechariah**

11:17, "Woe to the idol shepherd that leaveth the flock! The sword shall be upon his arm, and upon his right eye: his arm shall be clean dried up, and his right eye shall be utterly darkened."

Are we bad "shepherds" if we are selfish unto ourselves and self-serving to the point where we consciously make the decision to ignore our "Great Commission" and refuse to preach and teach the truth in favor of money and popularity? Our Lord answers this query in **Ezekiel 34:2,10, "... Woe be to the shepherds of Israel that do feed themselves! Should not the shepherds feed the flocks?... Thus saith the Lord God; Behold, I am against the shepherds."** Are we bad "shepherds" if we only lookout for ourselves, compare what we have to those around us and live according to secular humanism, materialism and relativism? God answers us forthrightly in **Isaiah 56:11 & 57:21; and in Titus 1:10-16; "Yea, they are greedy dogs which can never have enough, and they are shepherds that cannot understand: they all look to their own way, every one for his gain, from his quarter. There is no peace, saith my God, to the wicked." "For there are many unruly and vain talkers and deceivers...Whose mouths must be stopped, who subvert whole houses, teaching things which they ought not, for filthy lucre's sake. One of their own, said, The Cretians are always liars, evil beasts, slow bellies. This witness is true. Wherefore rebuke them sharply, that they may be sound in faith; Not giving heed to Jewish fables, and commandments of men, that turn from the truth. Unto the pure all things are pure: but unto them that are defiled and unbelieving is nothing pure; but even their mind and conscience is defiled. They profess that they know God; but in works they deny Him, being abominable, and disobedient, and unto every good work reprobate."**

Fellow Christians, let us resolve to be good "shepherds." Almighty God takes our "Great Commission" very seriously — it behooves us to do the same! We need to decide to be like Jesus. We need to decide to demonstrate Jesus to the lost and dying world. We need to decide to govern our lives according to His Word — Jesus Christ the Righteous. For the sake of Christ Jesus, let us summon the empowerment of the Holy Spirit so that we are enabled to "shepherd" Christ's sheep. Let us be mindful of the example as set by

David, another good "shepherd" of whom Jesus was a direct descendant. **"I am the root and offspring of David, and the bright and morning star." (Revelation 22:16 KJV).** **"And David said unto Saul, thy servant kept his father's sheep, and there came a lion and a bear, and took a lamb out of the flock: And I went out after him, and smote him, and delivered it out of his mouth." (1 Samuel 17:34,35 KJV).**

My friends in Christ, in **John 21:17**, Jesus commands us to, **"Feed My sheep"**. Scripture is replete with examples of Christ as the "Good Shepherd." You and I claim to be saved by the blood of the Lamb. You and I claim to follow Christ Jesus. You and I claim to be disciples of our Lord and Savior. You and I must execute our "Great Commission" for the sake of Christ Jesus. If we fail to live our "Great Commission", we are in direct disobedience to our Lord's command. If we fail to evangelize Jesus Christ, we are traitors to our God. If we fail to disciple on behalf of our Christ, we have betrayed and forsaken His Victory over the adversary, sin, death, sickness, oppression by evil spirits, possession by evil spirits, false preachers, prophets, and teachers in the apostate church, and the ways of the world. **"And whosoever doth not bear his cross, and come after Me, cannot be My disciple." (Luke 14:27 KJV).** O saints, let us choose to trust and obey our "Great Commission". Let us choose to do the honorable and good work of Jesus Christ! **"Now the God of peace that brought again from the dead our Lord Jesus, that Great Shepherd of the sheep, through the blood of the everlasting covenant, Make you perfect in every good work to do His will, working in you that which is well-pleasing in His sight, through Jesus Christ; to whom be glory for ever and ever Amen." (Hebrews 13:20,21 KJV).**

We are the overseers of Jesus' flock on this earth. We are chosen to lead others to salvation for the sake of Jesus. We are chosen to protect and defend — even die for our great "Cause for Christ". We are chosen to be His "shepherds" — His "Good Shepherds", and our "Great Commission" is to share the Gospel with all of mankind. We are chosen to grow and nurture Christ's Church — His Body — His Kingdom on this earth. We are chosen to be ever vigilant and to heed that still small voice of the Holy Spirit and demonstrate active, violent faith to win souls for Christ! **"Take heed therefore unto yourselves and to all the flock, over which the Holy Ghost has made you overseers, to feed the Church of God, which He hath purchased with His own blood." (Acts 20:28 KJV).**

Being a Christian in the truest sense of the word is a full time endeavor — it is a lifestyle. Whether it be with our families, at church or in the marketplace, we must be ever cognizant of and then demonstrate our responsibility to Jesus Christ and our "Great Commission". Let us remember what Christ sacrificed on our behalf — His very life. Let us remember the excruciating agony Jesus suffered for you and me — and to the eternal glory of Almighty God. Fellow "Conquerors for Christ", let us hereby highly resolve to advance Jesus Christ's Army of the Light, activate our "Great Commission" and be the good "Shepherds for Christ" that Christ has chosen us to be! As we mobilize the great body of Christ to overcome the enemy and win back the world for Christ, let us prayerfully consider the advice and counsel of the apostle Peter; **"The elders which are among you I exhort, who am also an elder, and a witness of the sufferings of Christ, and also a partaker of the glory that shall be revealed: Feed the flock of God which is among you, taking the oversight thereof, not by constraint, but willingly; not for filthy lucre, but of a ready mind; Neither as being lords over God's heritage, but being examples to the flock. And when the Chief Shepherd shall appear, ye shall receive a crown of glory that fadeth not away." (1 Peter 5:1-4 KJV). "For ye were as sheep going astray; but are now returned unto the Shepherd and Bishop of your souls." (1 Peter 2:25 KJV).**

> **"But they that wait upon the Lord shall renew their strength; they shall mount up with wings as eagles; they shall run, and not be weary; and they shall walk, and not faint." (Isaiah 40:31 KJV).**

Valor in Humility

"If My people, which are called by My Name, shall humble themselves, and pray, and seek My face, and turn from their wicked ways; then will I hear them from Heaven, and will forgive their sin, and will heal their land." (2 Chronicles 7:14 KJV). "For thus saith the high and lofty One that inhabiteth eternity, whose Name is Holy; I dwell in the high and holy place, with him also that is of a contrite and humble spirit, to revive the spirit of the humble, and to revive the heart of the contrite ones." (Isaiah 57:15 KJV).

Valor is bravery. Valor is courage and forthrightness. Valor is power and strength. Valor is the stuff of a hero. The questions become whether Christians can demonstrate valor while remaining humble? Or, in the alternative, are the terms mutually exclusive? "The meek will He guide in judgment: and the meek will He teach His way." (Psalm 25:9 KJV). "Blessed are the poor in spirit: for theirs is the Kingdom of Heaven." (Matthew 5:3 KJV). "Blessed are the meek: for they shall inherit the earth." (Matthew 5:5 KJV).

Let us prayerfully consider the word humility. What does it mean to be humble? The secular world's definition connotes a degrading characteristic — one who is preoccupied with one's defects or shortcomings. It contemplates a very weak, unassertive nature of little or no positive consequence — a person who is spiritless and spineless. According to this definition, the phrase "Valor in Humility" constitutes an oxymoron.

Praise God that His definition of humility — the true definition of humility — is much more compelling than that of the worlds, for God's ways are higher than our ways! Almighty God's definition of humility — His very example of humility — comes in the form of His only begotten Son, our Lord and Savior Jesus Christ! Therefore, humility is the hallmark of the Kingdom of God! Hallelujah! **"For as the heavens are higher than the earth, so are My ways higher than your ways, and My thoughts than your thoughts." (Isaiah 55:9 KJV). "Come unto Me, all ye that labor and are heavy laden, and I will give you rest. Take My yoke upon you, and learn of Me; for I am meek and lowly in heart: and ye shall find rest unto your souls. For My yoke is easy, and My burden is light." (Matthew 11:28-30 KJV).**

No one can argue that Christ Jesus demonstrated a weak, unassertive nature, or that His life produced little or no positive consequence, or that He was a person who was spiritless and spineless. Jesus was very bold and assertive about His Father's work. Jesus was filled with the Holy Spirit and stood strong in the face of overwhelming opposition. Jesus' life had supreme consequences — He revolutionized, revived and reconciled the world unto eternal glory with the Father! Indeed, Jesus is the ONLY WAY to God the Father! **"...I set My face like a flint..." (Isaiah 50:7 KJV). "For if, when we were enemies, we were reconciled to God by the death of His Son, much more, being reconciled, we shall be saved by His life." (Romans 5:10 KJV). "...I am the Way, the Truth and the Life: no man cometh unto the Father, but by Me." (John 14:6 KJV).**

Almighty God's definition of humility then, eschews the secular definition. God's definition of humility contemplates power and strength, which is disciplined by the wisdom of the Holy Spirit. It is the strength which is ultimately born from knowledge of, and faith in, the Word of God, and honed by our experiences which provide the necessary discipline in God's own wisdom. Thus, God's humility is disciplined power and strength, which comes from His wisdom and is never bitter, envious, boastful, driven by selfish ambition, nor manifested by denying the truth. Such character traits are of earthly wisdom and are unspiritual, emanating from Satan — that is why the spoiled fruits of said traits are disorder, division and evil practices.

"Who is a wise man and endued with knowledge among you? let him show out of a good conversation his works with meekness of wisdom. But if ye have bitter envying and strife in your hearts, glory not, and lie not against the truth. This wisdom descendeth not from above, but is earthly, sensual, devilish. For where envying and strife is, there is confusion and every evil work." (James 3:13-16 KJV).

God's definition of humility is further delineated by the disciplines of trust and faithful obedience which are obtained through suffering, while demonstrating a servant's heart and waiting in patience for God to exalt and/or to promote. God's humility NEVER glorifies self or presumes to say, "God told me, I am the one to have this position". Only through faithful obedience, steadfastness, perseverance and standing strong with all boldness on God's promises, and NOT running from the battle, thus deserting God's cause, can the humility of Jesus Christ be realized. We must ever aspire to have the same mind as Christ Jesus, trusting and faithfully obeying our heavenly Father, no matter what the price. **"Let this mind be in you, which was also in Christ Jesus. Who, being in the form of God, thought it not robbery to be equal with God. But made Himself of no reputation, and took upon Him the form of a servant, and was made in the likeness of men: And being found in fashion as a man, He humbled Himself, and became obedient unto death, even the death of the cross. Wherefore God also hath highly exalted Him, and given Him a Name which is above every name. That at the Name of Jesus every knee should bow, of things in heaven, and things in earth, and things under the earth. And that every tongue should confess that Jesus Christ is Lord, to the glory of God the Father."** (Philippians 2:5-11 KJV). **"Though He were a Son, yet learned He obedience by the things which He suffered; And being made perfect He became the Author of eternal salvation unto all them that obey Him; Called of God a High Priest after the order of Melchizedek."** (Hebrews 5:8-10 KJV).

A person of true humility holds himself or herself out to others in a selfless fashion. A person of true humility is meek, meaning patient and longsuffering, endeavoring to generate power through others. A person of true humility is engaged in the unselfish and constant pursuit of a common purpose — one in spirit (esprit de corps), esteeming others higher than, and considering the interests of others above, his or her own. **"Fulfill ye my joy, that ye be likeminded, having the same love, being of one accord, of one mind. Let nothing be done through strife or vainglory: but in lowliness of mind let each esteem other better than themselves. Look not every man on his own things, but every man also on the things of others."** (Philippians 2:2-4 KJV).

A person of true humility is NEVER manipulative — attempting to influence with the intent to deceive — be it in finding fault with others to aggrandize oneself in an effort to gain unfair advantage — or by cajoling, flattering and conning with the intent to slander, swindle or place oneself in a preferred position at the expense of others. A person of true humility NEVER pretends to be a loyal ally, confidant and friend, nor feigns doing the work he or she is assigned to do. A person of true humility has a pure and ethical heart. **"The wicked, through the pride of his countenance, will not seek after God: God is not in all his thoughts."** (Psalm 10:4 KJV). **"These six things doth the Lord hate: yea, seven are an abomination unto Him: A proud look, a lying tongue, and hands that shed innocent blood, A heart that deviseth wicked imaginations, feet that be swift in running to mischief, A false witness that speaketh lies, and he that soweth discord among brethren."** (Proverbs 6:16-19 KJV). **"The heart is deceitful above all things, and desperately wicked: who can know it? I the Lord search the heart, I try the reins, even to give every man according to his ways, and according to the fruit of his doings."** (Jeremiah 17:9,10 KJV).

The humility of Jesus Christ is to defer to and obey the authority under whom one is placed, unless said person is in unrepentant sin. It is a humility, which demonstrates a security in oneself through the Holy Spirit to be the servant-leader of others. It involves leading by example and becoming vulnerable to those around you — even unto betrayal. **"So after He had washed their feet, and had taken His garments, and was set down again, He said unto them, Know ye what I have done to you? Ye call Me Master and Lord: and** ye say well; for so I am. If I then, your Lord and Master, have washed your feet; ye also ought to wash one another's feet. For I have given you an example, that ye should do as I have done to you. Verily, verily, I say unto you, The servant is not greater than his lord; neither he that is sent greater than he that sent him. If ye know these things, happy are ye if ye do them." (John 13:12-17 KJV). "But Jesus said unto him, Judas, betrayest thou the Son of man with a kiss? (Luke 22:48 KJV).

The humility of Christ is that of a mentor–student relationship — a leader-subordinate scenario. There are significant risks involved with the ever-present temptation of the student choosing to demonstrate the satanic power of false pride and egoism to the extent that the student attempts to subvert the mentor to satisfy the egocentric nature of the student. As well, often it is the mentor who becomes jealous of the student. Because of the insecurity of the mentor, who has not yielded to the Spirit of God, he succumbs to the spirit of pride and jealousy, which leads to his/her ultimate destruction, as is witnessed in the demise of King Saul. This should NEVER occur between and among Christians — what kind of false witness would be bear by demonstrating this covetous behavior? God would NEVER tell someone to move in an ungodly fashion. What has become of being convicted in one's heart and spirit by the Holy Spirit? The Holy Spirit would NEVER tell a Christian to sin. It is a sad commentary that this phenomenon happens all too often within the body of Christ — in churches, in ministries and in the marketplace. I pray that, as Christians, we summon the wherewithal from the Holy Spirit to bind and cast down as part of Jesus' footstool the demons of false pride and egoism once and for all, by the blood of Jesus Christ and in the Name of Jesus Christ! Amen. Let us understand this truth — that humility always sees the weakness in pride — but pride never sees the strength in humility. **"And whosoever shall exalt himself shall be abased, and he that shall humble himself shall be exalted." (Matthew 23:12 KJV). "Woe to the crown of pride." (Isaiah 28:1 KJV). "Pride goeth before destruction, and a haughty spirit before a fall." (Proverbs 16:18 KJV). "...Therefore Saul took a sword and fell upon it...So Saul died, and his three sons, and his armor bearer, and all his men,**

that same day together." (1 Samuel 31:4, 6 KJV). If we do not turn away from the idols of false pride, egocentrism, slander and manipulation in favor of true, other-centered Christ-like humility, then our punishment shall be like unto that declared in **Deuteronomy 8:19,20, "And it shall be, if thou do at all forget the Lord thy God, and walk after other gods, and serve them, and worship them, I testify against you this day that ye shall surely perish. As the nations which the Lord destroyeth before your face so shall ye perish; because ye would not be obedient unto the voice of the Lord your God."**

My friends in Christ, the record is clear — there is great bravery in the humility of Christ. There is great courage and forthrightness in the humility of Christ. There is great authority, power and strength in the humility of Christ. There is great heroism in the humility of Christ. Hence, there is great "Valor In Humility"! **"I am crucified with Christ: nevertheless I live; yet not I, but Christ liveth in me: and the life which I now live in the flesh I live by the faith of the Son of God, who loved me, and gave Himself for me." (Galatians 2:20 KJV). "I can do all things through Christ which strengtheneth me." (Philippians 4:13 KJV).**

Let us highly resolve to humble ourselves before the Lord and completely trust and faithfully obey Him, exclusively. Let us highly resolve to humbly and willingly endure suffering in order to be fashioned, honed and molded by our God for His high service while demonstrating perseverance and patience — waiting on Him to exalt us. Let us highly resolve to be bold, yet humble, in our proclamation of the Gospel via the marketplace and beyond, in our daily lives. Let us highly resolve to humbly assert and demonstrate Jesus Christ to this lost and dying world. Let us highly resolve to humbly practice being people of the Holy Spirit — full of and living in the very Spirit of Christ -- and demonstrating His courage and willpower, in the mighty Name of Jesus Christ. Let us highly resolve to be humbly and eternally vigilant regarding our evil adversary! **"Humble yourselves therefore under the mighty hand of God, that He may exalt you in due time: Casting all your care upon Him; for He careth for you. Be sober, be vigilant; because your adversary the devil, as a roaring lion, walketh about, seeking** whom he may devour: Whom resist steadfast in the faith, knowing that the same afflictions are accomplished in your brethren that are in the world. But the God of all grace, who hath called us unto his eternal glory by Christ Jesus, after that ye have suffered a while, make you perfect, stablish, strengthen, settle you. To Him be glory and dominion for ever and ever. Amen." (1 Peter 5:6-11 KJV).

Let us highly resolve to humbly execute and live God's holy wisdom, which flows from the Holy Spirit. Let us highly resolve to humbly serve others and pursue our "Great Commission" to the glory of Almighty God in the marketplace and beyond, in our daily lives. Let us highly resolve to diligently demonstrate our allegiance to Jesus Christ by activating our violent faith with humble virtue, boldness, kindness and love. "...[T]he Kingdom of Heaven suffereth violence, and the violent take it by force." (Matthew 11:12 KJV). "And beside this, giving all diligence, add to your faith virtue; and to virtue knowledge; And to knowledge temperance; and to temperance patience; and to patience godliness; And to godliness brotherly kindness; and to brotherly kindness charity." (2 Peter 1:5-7 KJV). Let it be written. Let it be done. Praise God!

"But they that wait upon the Lord shall renew their strength; they shall mount up with wings as eagles; they shall run, and not be weary; and they shall walk, and not faint." (Isaiah 40:31 KJV).

Christ's Character Is Our Destiny

Those of us who "claim" to be Christians need to sincerely and prayerfully examine ourselves as to our true character, on a daily basis. Character is one's overall excellence, moral constitution and moral strength — as relating to the capability of making the distinction between right and wrong conduct and then acting upon said righteous conduct. Character involves the notion of fortitude — the strength to bear misfortune, pain, et al, calmly and patiently, while demonstrating firm courage and resolve. Character is all about exemplary Jesus-discipline in the face of extreme opposition and unfavorable circumstances. Character means that we possess the wherewithal to "stay the course" in the jaws of adversity, remaining loyal and steadfast to Jesus Christ, our family, colleagues, leaders and fellow soldiers in Christ's Army of the Light. **"For we know that all things work together for good to them that love God, to them who are the called according to His purpose. For whom He did foreknow, He also did predestinate to be conformed to the image of His Son, that He might be the first-born among many brethren." (Romans 8:28, 29 KJV). "Now the Lord is that Spirit: and where the Spirit of the Lord is, there is liberty. But we all, with open face beholding as in a glass the glory of the Lord, are changed into the same image from glory to glory, even as by the Spirit of the Lord." (2 Corinthians 3:17, 18 KJV). "For I reckon that the sufferings of this present time are not worthy to be compared with the glory which shall be revealed in us." (Romans 8:18 KJV).** Character does NOT accuse or blame anyone for our condition, rather it rests in the knowledge that a loving Sovereign God is still on the throne. Character means being like

Jesus Christ. When we have character, Jesus Christ becomes our essential quality. **"My heart is fixed, O God, my heart is fixed: I will sing and give praise." (Psalm 57:7 KJV). "And ye shall be hated of all men for My Name's sake: but he that endureth to the end shall be saved." (Matthew 10:22 KJV).**

Let us ask the following questions of ourselves and answer them honestly, before the cross of Christ. Am I actively or passively engaging in an ongoing quest of sedition — the clandestine, insidious and nefarious stirring up of discontent, doubt, resistance — even rebellion against God's anointed people and/or work? **"Saying, Touch not Mine anointed, and do My prophets no harm." (Psalm 105:15 KJV).** Am I committing the overt act of treason against the same — the betraying of the trust and faith — the violation of the sacred allegiance to which I have pledged? Have I ever participated in harmful gossip and slander, or called someone aside and said, " this is just between you and me", or "this conversation never happened", and then proceeded to plant seeds of fear, doubt, discontent, innuendo, et al? If you are a person of character, the answer to the aforementioned queries is a resounding "NO"! If you are a person who lacks character, the unhappy answer is "YES". If the answer is yes, then said actions of sedition and treason are being committed against Christ Jesus, Himself. **"They also that seek after My life lay snares for Me; and they that seek My hurt speak mischievous things, and imagine deceits all the day long." (Psalm 38:12 KJV). "Now he that betrayed Him gave them a sign, saying, Whomsoever I shall kiss, that same is He: hold Him fast. And forthwith he came to Jesus, and said, Hail, Master; and kissed Him. And Jesus said unto him, Friend, wherefore art thou come? Then came they, and laid hands on Jesus, and took Him." (Matthew 26:48-50 KJV).**

I realize that these issues are hard-hitting — and rightfully so. The business in which we are engaged — winning souls to everlasting salvation in Christ Jesus — is the most serious of all. Sedition, slander and treason within the Body of Christ must not be tolerated. Could it be that many of us who "claim" to be Christians demonstrate the ways of the apostasy — heretics — hypocrites — accusers — blamers — blasphemers — false preachers, prophets and teachers — even traitors? If this applies, then the Bible asserts that Jesus Christ does not live within us — else we surely would not live such ways. **"This know also, that in the last days perilous times shall come. For men shall be lovers of their own selves, covetous, boasters, proud, blasphemers, disobedient to parents, unthankful, unholy. Without natural affection, trucebreakers, false accusers, incontinent, fierce, despisers of those that are good, Traitors, heady, high-minded, lovers of pleasures more than lovers of God; Having a form of godliness, but denying the power thereof: from such turn away."** (2 Timothy 3:1-5 KJV). The time is nigh that we — as the Body of Christ — need to live the character of our leader, Jesus Christ, because "Christ's Character Is Our Destiny"! **"And they were both righteous before God, walking in all the commandments and ordinances of the Lord blameless."** (Luke 1:6 KJV).

Destiny is the course, the purpose, the vision and the goals to which we are bound and chosen to attain — in our case — to be holy saints on this earth. To be holy means to have the divine quality of Christ Jesus. It necessarily follows that, if our character does not embody Jesus Christ as our essential quality, then we fall short of our destiny. The good news is that, once we genuinely accept Christ as our Lord and Savior and commit our lives to living His character, God's mighty work in us begins to manifest in many ways to build Christ's very character within us. Everything we experience should be turned into Christ's character. God will place us through rigorous circumstances to develop our faith — the faith that is tried and true — the faith that has stood the test. **"But He knoweth the way that I take: when He hath tried me, I shall come forth as gold."** (Job 23:10 KJV). **"But thou, O man of God, flee these things; and follow after righteousness, godliness, faith, love, patience, meekness. Fight the good fight of faith, lay hold on eternal life, whereunto thou art also called, and hast professed a good profession before many witnesses."** (1 Timothy 6:11, 12 KJV). Our growth in character purifies our faith, thus the character to which we aspire is the character to be worthy to be "called, and chosen, and faithful." **"These shall make war with the Lamb, and the Lamb shall overcome them: for he is Lord of lords, and King** of kings: and they that are with him are called, and chosen and faithful." (Revelation 17:14 KJV).

The Holy Spirit, as our Comforter, teaches us all of the divine qualities of Christ Jesus, including perseverance and persistence — to be overcomers in Jesus' mighty Name, no matter what circumstances we face. He helps build our personal character as the Word of God reveals His Knowledge unto us. Armed with the knowledge of God through His Word and Divine Revelation, He then imparts His Divine Wisdom via our various experiences in life. Our goal is consummate focus on Christ Jesus — exclusively — so that we are able to acquire and then live up to His Vision — the "Great Commission". Our character must be that of making moral choices that are contrary to the secular world. We must eschew any notion of apostasy, sedition and treason within the Body of Christ. These diabolical ways of Satan must be avoided lest we fall prey to the enemy's snares. The WAY to overcome is The WAY of the cross of Christ. **"I am crucified with Christ: nevertheless I live; yet not I, but Christ liveth in me: and the life which I now live in the flesh I live by the faith of the Son of God, who loved me, and gave Himself for me." Galatians 2:20 KJV). "And He said to them all, If any man will come after Me, let him deny himself and take up his cross daily, and follow Me." (Luke 9:23 KJV).** We must be men and women after God's own heart. **". . . the Lord hath sought Him a man after His own heart, and the Lord hath commanded him to be captain over His people." (1 Samuel 13:14 KJV).**

Our destiny, then, is to always hear God's still small voice — to discern His will by the power of His Holy Spirit. Many of us who are chosen for high service find ourselves descending into greatness. We reach a pinnacle in our lives according to secular standards and then we lose it all for the sake of Christ. This is the very stuff of the character of Christ — accept it to the glory of God and He will make you a great "Conqueror for Christ"! **"For Thou, O God, hast proved us: Thou hast tried us, as silver is tried." (Psalm 66:10 KJV). "But what things were gain to me, those I counted loss for Christ. Yea doubtless, and I count all things but loss for the exellency of the knowledge of Christ Jesus my Lord: for whom I have suffered the loss of all things, and do count them but dung,** that I may win Christ." (Philippians 3:7, 8 KJV). Our destiny — our holiness (the divine quality of Christ Jesus — our essence) comes from a perfect union with Almighty God through Christ's atoning death and glorious Resurrection. Thus, our destiny — our holiness is manifested through our character — the character and image of Christ in us — as we bear the fruit of the Holy Spirit. Truly, "Christ's Character is Our Destiny!" **"Because it is written, BE YE HOLY; FOR I AM HOLY." (1 Peter 1:16 KJV). "But the fruit of the Spirit is love, joy, peace, long-suffering, gentleness, goodness, faith, Meekness, temperance: against such there is no law." (Galatians 5:22, 24 KJV).**

Fellow "Conquerors for Christ", the only WAY we are able to live and demonstrate our "Great Commission" is to live the character of Christ. As we foster and propagate Christ's Gospel to our neighborhoods, commerce centers and throughout the world, let us know and understand that Jesus Christ needs to be our essential quality — our very character — in order for us to be successful soldiers in His Army of the Light. In order for us to be shining examples of our Lord and Savior we must be of His mind and heart, and demonstrate esprit de corps and oneness in the body of Christ. Then, and only then, will we be successful in enforcing His Victory over Satan and being overcomers for Christ. Let us be ever mindful of the severe consequences of sedition and treason in time of war — the ultimate consequence is death. We are engaged in the war of all wars — the war against Satan to save souls for Christ Jesus. The war we wage is spiritual and lasts for eternity. How much more severe are the consequences of sedition and treason? **"But the fearful, and unbelieving, and the abominable, and murderers, and whoremongers, and sorcerers, and idolaters, and all liars, shall have their part in the lake which burneth with fire and brimstone: which is the second death." (Revelation 21:8 KJV).**

Fellow "Conquerors for Christ", let us hereby resolve to be of the same mind of Christ. **"Let this mind be in you, which was also in Christ Jesus." (Philippians 2:5 KJV).** Our Lord and Savior would never contemplate sedition or treason — why would we? **"Now I beseech you, brethren, by the Name of our Lord Jesus Christ, that ye all speak the same thing, and that there be no divisions** among you: but that ye be perfectly joined together in the same mind and in the same judgment." (1 Corinthians 1:10 KJV). Let us choose holiness by drawing nigh unto Almighty God so that He may purify our hearts — that we may truly be the unified, ever advancing Army of the Light of Jesus Christ! **"Draw nigh to God, and he will draw nigh to you. Cleanse your hands, ye sinners; and purify your hearts, ye doubleminded." (James 4:8 KJV).**

Let us be the enforcers of Christ's Victory over the enemy, sin, false preachers, prophets and teachers in the apostate church, and the ways of the world! Let us be Christ's overcomers here on this earth! Let us, once and for all, stake our "claim" in Christ and live as our Lord and Savior would have us live! We are able to accomplish this by unconditionally accepting our circumstances with the joy of Christ. Let us celebrate our sufferings and difficult times to the glory of Christ Jesus. In so doing, we allow God to build in us the very character of Christ — for "Christ's Character Is Our Destiny"! **"For whatsoever is born of God overcometh the world: and this is the victory that overcometh the world, even our faith. Who is he that overcometh the world, but he that believeth that Jesus is the Son of God?" (1 John 5:4, 5 KJV).**

> **"But they that wait upon the Lord shall renew their strength; they shall mount up with wings as eagles; they shall run, and not be weary; and they shall walk, and not faint." (Isaiah 40:31 KJV).**

COMMITMENT TO ACTION

⤞

I HEREBY HIGHLY RESOLVE AND COVENANT BEFORE MY LORD AND SAVIOR JESUS CHRIST, MY FAMILY, MY FELLOW CHRISTIANS AND SOLDIERS OF THE CROSS OF JESUS CHRIST THAT, ONGOING, I AM SUMMONING THE NECESSARY COURAGE AND EMPOWERMENT THROUGH THE POWER OF THE HOLY SPIRIT, TO BE AN EVANGELIST AND DISCIPLE OF JESUS CHRIST BY LIVING HIS DISCIPLINE, INTEGRITY AND CHARACTER. I AM ASSERTING ALL OF THE KINGDOM AUTHORITY AND POWER OF CHRIST JESUS AGAINST THE ENEMY, SIN, FALSE PEACHERS, PROPHETS AND TEACHERS IN THE APOSTATE CHURCH, AND THE WAYS OF THE WORLD, THEREBY ENFORCING HIS VICTORY. I AM HONORING HIM AND EXERCISING MY FREEDOM AND LIBERTY IN HIM, BY DUTIFULLY AND DILGENTLY, EXECUTING AND FULFILLING THE SHARED VISION HE HAS BESTOWED UPON ME VIA HIS "GREAT COMMISSION". I AM CONTENDING FOR, CONFIRMING AND DEFENDING THE FAITH AND THE GOSPEL, AT EVERY TURN. I AM LIVING AND PREACHING THE CROSS OF CHRIST AND THE POWER OF HIS RESURRECTION. I AM HIS KING AND HIS PRIEST IN THE MARKETPLACE AND BEYOND, IN MY DAILY LIFE! I AM DEMONSTRATING "LEADERSHIP -- SHOWING 'THE WAY" TO SALVATION BY SHARING THE GOSPEL OF JESUS CHRIST EVERY DAY WITH MY FELLOW MEN, WOMEN AND CHILDREN IN MY SPHERE OF INFLUENCE, AS WELL AS AROUND THE WHOLE OF THE WORLD. I AM

AN EXECUTOR, STEWARD AND TRUSTEE OF THE LAST WILL AND TESTAMENT OF MY LORD AND SAVIOR JESUS CHRIST -- HIS GOSPEL! I AM A "CONQUEROR FOR CHRIST"! AMEN! HALLELUJAH!

MY SIGNITURE   DATE

"...All power is given unto Me in heaven and in earth. Go ye therefore, and teach all nations, baptizing them in the name of the Father, and of the Son, and of the Holy Ghost: Teaching them to observe all things whatsoever I have commanded you: and, lo, I am with you always, even unto the end of the world. Amen." (Matthew 28:18-20 KJV). "Go ye into all the world, and preach the Gospel to every creature." (Mark 16:15 KJV).

"For whom He did foreknow, He also did predestinate to be conformed to the image of His Son..." (Romans 8:29 KJV).

"Now the Lord is that Spirit: and where the Spirit of the Lord is, there is liberty. But we all, with open face beholding as in a glass the glory of the Lord, are changed into the same image from glory to glory, even as by the Spirit of the Lord." (2 Corinthians 3:17, 18 KJV).

"And hath made us kings and priests unto God and His Father; to Him be glory and dominion for ever and ever. Amen." "And hast made us unto our God kings and priests: and we shall reign on the earth." (Revelation 1:6; 5:10 KJV).

"...[T]he Kingdom of Heaven suffereth violence, and the violent take it by force." (Matthew 11:12 KJV).

"Behold, I give you power to tread on serpents and scorpions, and over all the power of the enemy: and nothing shall by any means hurt you." (Luke 10:19 KJV).

"But thanks be to God which giveth us the victory through our Lord Jesus Christ." (1 Corinthians 15:57 KJV).

"I can do all things through Christ which strengtheneth me." (Philippians 4:13 KJV).

"For the preaching of the cross...is the power of God." (1 Corinthians 1:18 KJV).

"...[A]nd in the defense and confirmation of the Gospel... I am set for the defense of the Gospel." (Philippians 1:7, 17 KJV).

"Beloved, when I gave all diligence to write unto you of the common salvation, it was needful for me to write unto you, and exhort you that ye should earnestly contend for the faith..." (Jude 3 KJV).

"According to the glorious Gospel of the blessed God, which was committed to my trust." (1 Timothy 1:11 KJV).

"O Timothy, keep that which is committed to thy trust, avoiding profane and vain babblings, and oppositions of science falsely so called: Which some professing have erred concerning the faith. Grace be with thee. Amen. " (1 Timothy 6:20, 21 KJV).

"Nay, in all these things we are more than conquerors through him that loved us." (Romans 8:37 KJV).

"But they that wait upon the Lord shall renew their strength; they shall mount up with wings as eagles; they shall run, and not be weary; and they shall walk, and not faint." (Isaiah 40:31 KJV).

Contact Us
&
In Re: Volume 2

For Crusades & Revivals, Preaching & Teaching

Contact:

God & Country Revival
1300 11th Ave. Suite 303
Altoona, Pa., 16601
814-942-1995
michael@ocwn.net
www.godandcountryrevival.com

Conquerors for Christ, Volume 2, Is in Process

We Entreat Your Prayers!

"Nay, in all these things we are more than conquerors through him that loved us." (Romans 8:37 KJV).

"Conquerors for Christ" Battle Cry:

"Give us souls lest we die, that the Lamb who was slain might receive the reward of his suffering, as the glory perfects the unity, and the unity proclaims the glory"! Amen!

Printed in the United States
59263LVS00005B/94-132